There are no unnatural
or supernatural phenomena,
only very large gaps in our knowledge
of what is natural...
We should strive to fill
those gaps of ignorance.

Edgar D. Mitchell, Apollo 14 Astronaut

Other Books in the Show Me Missouri Series:

Missouri Ghosts

Joan Gilbert

Pebble Publishing
Columbia, Missouri

Project support by Pebble Publishing staff:
Addie Adams, R.C. Adams, Scott Angus, Brian Beatte, Tawnee Brown, Brett Dufur, Daisy Dufur, Jeff Lehman, Pippa Letsky and Hope Wagner

ISBN 0-9646625-7-4 14.95

Pebble Publishing, P.O. Box 431, Columbia, MO 65205-0431
Phone: 1 (800) 576-7322 • Fax: (573) 698-3108
E-Mail: Pebble@showmestate.com
Online: Katytrail.showmestate.com & Trailsidebooks.com

Printed by Ovid Bell Press, Fulton, Missouri, USA

Contents

Preface

Drifting fog...threatening thunder...a crumbling castle or dark old mansion, and nearby a solitary traveler who has lost his way. Then scudding clouds extinguish faint moonlight and the traveler sees...or hears...or feels...

These are standard ingredients of ghost stories, but we usually picture them in Europe, or perhaps on the East Coast, where our oldest buildings stand. We don't really expect to find spooks in good old Missouri—not beside our lovely streams, our tranquil woods, in our cozy little towns or in our modern cities.

Yet we have more than our share of ghostly doings. According to Beth Scott and Michael Norman, who compiled four books of American ghost stories, Missouri and Illinois are especially rich in reports of supernatural activity. The writers believe this is so because many settlers brought with them the British Isles tradition of storytelling and because, unknowingly or uncaringly, they disturbed burial sites sacred to many generations of Native Americans. This must have released multitudes of confused or resentful spirits, judging from the number of Missourians who have a few good tales, usually sworn to by relatives or trusted friends.

Collecting and sharing our ghost stories is a writer's dream because nobody expects documentation. The closest thing we can hope for as proof is when two or more people experience something together and agree to be quoted about it. Most often, they agree to tell their story only after certain conditions of anonymity are met, such as not mentioning their names or hometowns. And photographs and recordings of ghosts mean little, since they are easily faked. Many apparent hauntings—including some described here—could easily be staged by someone clever and agile. It's indisputable that stress, some illnesses and some medications can cause hallucinations—visual, auditory and olfactory.

So the whole issue of whether or not ghosts exist is like the everlasting debate on whether or not animals have reasoning power and souls. Who can prove the contrary? Perhaps no one has ever dealt with ghosts better than Shakespeare, in *Hamlet*, with the famous line: "There are more things in heaven and earth, Horatio, than are dreamt of in your philosophy."

Missouri has two great unexplained mysteries, the case of Patience Worth and the matter of the Spook Light, visible near the small town of Hornet. Counting Jim the Wonder Dog and real events upon which the *The Exorcist* book and movie were based, we have four enigmas that have attracted to our state—and continue to attract—serious students of the paranormal. Missouri also has three residents with national status among psychic investigators and writers in the field. These investigators include Bevy Jaegers of St. Louis, Maurice Schwalm of Kansas City and Dr. Irene Hickman of Kirksville. They can tell us what ghosts probably really are, and what to do when we meet them.

Only one thing more: this book does not pretend to present full or equitable coverage of Missouri's ghosts; it contains only what came to one person's attention. Readers may send their own stories to Pebble Publishing for possible use in future editions of *Missouri Ghosts*.

Joan Gilbert

Chapter One

Neighborhood Ghosts

My mother saw a ghost and always considered it one of the nicest experiences of her life. It happened one afternoon in the 1920s, when she was lying across her bed crying about some temporary crisis, and suddenly found herself looking at a favorite aunt who had died years before.

"Why I thought you were dead!" she exclaimed, amazed to be more delighted than frightened.

The aunt said nothing. She only smiled and shook her head, but in such a loving, comforting, encouraging way that her message was unmistakable: "Death is not like you think...nothing is really so bad...everything will be fine for you...don't cry."

This brief encounter gave my mother strength for her lifetime. Hearing her story often was a cherished part of my childhood. I loved the details she remembered: Her aunt, who had died in old age of a ravaging disease, appeared "young and rested," her expression serene. Her simple, cream-colored garment seemed somehow as thick as wool and as delicate as silk.

He talked and as he talked

Wallpaper came alive;

Suddenly ghosts walked...

Mark Van Doren, "The Story Teller"

My mother's story is one of several stories I heard as a child from relatives and neighbors. Recalling them always evokes a delicious sense of fascinating danger kept safely at bay by familiar surroundings and the presence of loving adults. The words "ghost story" bring back our front porch at night, Cousin Lizzie's cozy kitchen, the smell of her husband's pipe tobacco and my urgency in pedaling home from their house before darkness fell.

In another story, our neighbor Minnie's brush with the hereafter was as happy as my mother's. Her experience occurred at the turn of the century when she was barely a teenager. She saw a recently deceased little brother for a few seconds, trailing along behind her other siblings.

"He was wearing his favorite hat and carrying his usual long 'poking stick', bouncing the end of it off the path in front of him as he always did," she said. "He was as solid as any of the others. It was broad daylight and the children were coming in because I had called them and they had heard me. I was not dreaming." To get to the gate, the children had to pass behind some lilacs which hid them for a moment. When they came out, Minnie said, "He wasn't with them."

Another neighbor told of looking up from her ironing one day to see on the wall an image of a brother who lived several states away. "It was like a portrait," she said, "in color, just from the chest up. He was looking out at me and smiling. He didn't move or say anything, but he looked so well and so happy, like in the best years of his life. He looked ready to speak."

Two days later, she learned of his death.

Like my mother's story, these experiences gave peace and strength, seeming to show that wherever they are, the departed can be safe and content.

Making a Choice

Here is a story I thought of every time I passed a certain house, less than a block from where I grew up.

One night in the 1920s, remnants of two families gathered after a double funeral to consider the future of an infant orphaned by the sudden deaths of a young couple. None present were of an age, or situated, to feel capable of rearing a child, but they agreed this one must not go to an orphanage. As they sat in silence, each no doubt hoping one of the others would offer, a faint ringing sound and vibration began to go around the circle, as if someone was moving from person to person, ringing a tiny bell over each head. "A crystal bell," one of the relatives told my mother, "or a little glass triangle, a lovely sound, very small, though everyone could hear it."

Twice the bell went around the circle. Then it stopped above an aging, unmarried woman who seemed the poorest possible choice. (She had few

Is it not wonderful

that 5,000 years have now elapsed

since the creation of the world,

and still it is undecided, whether or not

there has even been an instance of the spirit

of any person appearing after death?

All argument is against it;

but all belief is for it.

Samuel Boswell, "Life of Johnson"

assets, just the house she lived in left to her by her parents, and a small income from dressmaking.) Nevertheless, she agreed to rear the child if others would help financially. They promised and kept their word; and this aunt, older than some of those present that night, was the only one still alive when the focus of their loving concern finished high school.

My mother often said, "Those parents knew who to call on."

The Well-Shod Ghost

A nother hometown story came from my mother's elderly friend, known to all as Grandma R. An immaculate little lady, her beautiful white hair made aging seem an enviable condition. At the corner of her property was a pear tree whose hearty growth raised and broke the sidewalk. I'm sure my mother and I were not the only people who ever walked up to that corner at night just to see pear blossoms in the moonlight.

Under this tree, just about dawn one day, Grandma R. told my mother she saw "a ghost or something." She had spent the night, sitting up in the old-fashioned way, with the wife of a man who was terminally ill. Grandma R. was tired, but, she declared, certainly not sleepwalking. She was in a peaceful frame of mind, having faith in her prayers that her neighbor would have an easy departure.

After her encounter under the tree, Grandma R. was not surprised, on going back to her friends' house, to find the husband had slipped away quietly in his sleep. "It must have been his spirit I saw, which paused to say goodbye and send me back to be with Martha...or maybe an angel, come to help him over," she told my mother. "But it didn't have wings." She described the being as not at all frightening; its face was sweet and its eyes looked kindly into hers. "I wouldn't say it was a man or a woman," she said, "but there was a sort of glimmer about it, and blonde hair." There was the white robe one expects for either ghost or angel, and one surprising item of attire. My mother used to smile at the puzzled way her friend would say, "I noticed in particular...imagine!...it had on white shoes!"

Accusing Footprints

O f all the people in my childhood, Lizzie's husband, Ed, was the best storyteller and the most interested in ghosts. He was a blacksmith and children were drawn to his shop, both to watch him work and to hear the tales he told. Even while holding up one-fourth of a horse, even while hammering red hot shoes into shape, he knew just when to lower his voice, just when to pause and say, "and what do you think happened then?"

I heard the pastor's words again,
"When the body wears away
like a car and can't go on,
the soul gets out and walks ahead
until it finds its home."

Bee Kuckelman, "Bonnie"

While driving the big nails in, to keep them handy, Ed held in his mouth the number he'd need for one shoe. Of course he couldn't talk then, and we had to wait. This somehow seemed always to coincide with the most suspenseful part of a tale.

It was from Ed that I heard my first disquieting ghost stories, and for one there was proof, which we could see when we visited him at home. Side by side at a bedroom window, he would show us the two distinct marks of bare feet, as if someone walked through the dew and peered into the house. No other prints came up the steps or across the porch however, but these two never dried up. Scrubbing only dimmed them. They were eventually painted over.

The footprints first appeared, Ed said, some twenty years earlier, while his aged mother lay dying several blocks away and one of his own children lay fatally ill (though nobody realized this at the time) just inside the window. Cousin Lizzie told my mother she was feeling guilty then, staying home to care for the child, whose illness everyone dismissed, while her mother-in-law undeniably needed help.

My friends and I rejected my father's remark that Ed probably made the tracks himself with kerosene. We debated other possibilities. Did the grandmother's spirit come reproachfully, to see why her stricken body was being neglected? Or, aware that they would enter the unknown within a week of each other, did her spirit come to accompany the child's? I still shiver, remembering the voices and tones of my elders discussing this.

What Did Dixie See?

Ed told another story for which I've found several variations, but none that is better. It made me look with new respect at my father's bird dogs, my constant companions. Could they maybe sense danger I couldn't see, and protect me with their warnings? Dogs often seem to have an active sixth sense when spirits are near, such as in the following story.

Ed said relatives were clearing out a large old house that had belonged to a recently deceased couple who'd lived there more than 50 years. The chore had taken a week already, and everyone had long since lost zeal for making sure that each useful item found the most appropriate individual or organization. One lady brought her dog along for company, since she had volunteered to do the attic and was finding it lonely up there.

The dog was named Dixie, a big old mixed-breed who had spent a great deal of time in the house from puppyhood, even visiting for weeks at a stretch when his owners traveled. His quiet presence was helpful, an island of total relaxation as he snoozed contentedly in a patch of sunlight

There is scarcely any other matter
upon which our thoughts and feelings
have changed so little
since the very earliest times.

Sigmund Freud, "The Uncanny"

from the now uncurtained attic window. One day Dixie changed. His owner didn't see what happened, or see the preliminary stages of his movement. She only turned, hearing a sound she described as "part whimper and part growl," to find Dixie flat on the floor, trembling, backed against the wall and looking up, past his owner, as if certain of attack from that direction.

When she said, "What's wrong, Dixie?" he turned his face slowly, with difficulty, and crept a step or two toward her. Then he seemed to suddenly gain enough courage to scramble past and down the stairs, rolling part way. She went out to find him cowering under the car, shaking violently.

"They said he shook for 45 minutes," Ed told us, relaying this story. "And he never went back in that house. He was even suspicious of the car for a month or more—even though he had loved riding and was always ready to go. This was a dog I knew, and if you ask me, he never was right again."

Nobody else who was in the house that day saw or heard anything unusual, and nobody ever had, so far as the family knew. No tragedies had taken place there. Though all agreed that Dixie was a sensible dog and something must have happened, they did not mention the incident to outsiders, lest they sound silly. People who bought the house loved it. Far from complaining about anything strange, they said they could feel the warm family life that had existed there previously.

My relatives and our friends told more stories than these, some of which they picked apart as possible practical jokes, or as delusions of someone who "always was a little flighty" or "under a lot of strain at that time." We were not familiar with psychological terms meaning the same thing and such buzzwords as "wishful thinking" were not yet in the language. Probably some of our stories could be dismissed that way: a young wife, feeling isolated with her problems is comforted by a loving aunt; and a young person, working through her first bereavement, assures herself that a little brother lost to her still lives happily in another dimension.

Whatever the truth of these stories, they opened my mind at a very early age to the fact that human certainty has severe limitations. These stories also demonstrated that we shouldn't believe everything everyone says. Other stories—collected over a lifetime and shared here—reinforced these lessons.

Chapter Two

Out in the County

One of Ed's stories concerned a family farther away, that he had known in his younger years. Ed felt especially strongly about them because their son had been of age to serve in World War I. It seems the young man in the family, against the wishes of his father who needed his help at home, set off to enlist when the United States went to war. He left home before daylight to walk several miles to town, carrying a lantern to light his way across the fields. He said he'd leave the lantern at the schoolhouse for the children to bring home after classes. His family never saw him or the lantern again, and never received even a letter from him.

What they did see, on certain summer nights, was a small swinging light, like a lantern in someone's hand, coming across the fields toward the house. The first time they saw it, they thought it was the lost son and ran joyously to meet him, calling his name. The light immediately disappeared. This happened to three generations of the family. Any calling out stopped the light at once, but even if no one spoke, it came only so close to the house before disappearing.

What beck'ning ghost...

Invites my steps...?

Alexander Pope, "Elegy to the Memory of an Unfortunate Lady"

Questions are obvious. Had the boy met with foul play while still in his own neighborhood? But it was a congenial, tight-knit community and neither he nor his family had enemies. If he'd been killed in the war, wouldn't the government have informed them? Had he used enlisting as an excuse to get away from home and met with misfortune that made him ashamed, though his spirit kept trying to return? The family couldn't believe he'd be so cruel as to leave them in suspense about his fate if he had any way at all of communicating.

So, is this re-occurring light just a natural phenomenon we don't understand yet? Some skeptics of ghostly sightings would agree. In fact, unusual lights are often reported at various places in the world. These phenomena are discussed in greater detail in Chapter 12.

The Misplaced Teen

Another lost person figures into a story carried by either the Waynesville or St. Robert newspaper in the 1960s. It came in the form of a letter to the editor from a couple who wished to remain anonymous, they said, for the sake of the value of property they'd sold in Pulaski County when they moved to another state. They wanted to speak out on something that might be of use to a particular pair of parents in the area.

The writers said that several times, in the hallway of their St. Robert home, they saw a pretty young girl, blonde, dressed in a short and modern blue dress, walking hastily away from them. Two or three times she turned, seemed to see them, paused, looking confused and frightened, then hurried out of sight. The couple, whose house had been built new for them, fronting a stretch of new highway, wondered if any girl fitting their description had died there, perhaps having been kidnapped or in a car wreck. They said that each time they saw her, they felt overpowering pity and wished they could do something to help her.

Later editorial comment said local law enforcement offices had no file on a missing young woman. This is typical of many ghost stories which give us no conclusion, only a mystery to puzzle over.

Ghostly Treasures

Three Pulaski County stories are classic. They all deal with fortunes abandoned due to sudden deaths. Two of them have inspired generations of treasure hunters.

The first story centers on a historic building in the Buckhorn community near Waynesville, which served as a stagecoach stop 120 years ago. Since then, the old inn has become a private dwelling. For Halloween in 1980,

if you had known

as many of them as I have,

you would not believe in them either.

Don Marquis, archy the cockroach poet

when its owners, Emerson and Marie Storie, were interviewed by a reporter for the *Gateway Guide*, they said they'd heard footsteps when no one was present but themselves. They also said they smelled hickory smoke where no fire existed. Their daughter, in an upstairs bedroom, said she often heard heavy breathing that might even, at times, be called agonized.

Marie Storie was quoted in the publication as saying "We're not superstitious, but there are things happening here that we just can't explain."

In one of the building's stories, three travelers from California checked in one stormy night, and foolishly discussed the gold they'd panned for and were now taking home for nest eggs. They soon became suspicious of the landlord's interest in them, however. They agreed that while two occupied his attention, the other would take their valises (small hand luggage popular in the 1800s) outdoors and hide them.

The wiley landlord caught on, but steady rain made it impossible to follow tracks or find where digging had occurred, so upstairs he cornered the one who'd buried the gold. When the traveler could not be easily coerced, the landlord turned to torture, threatening the miner with a glowing poker heated in the fire. The landlord was thwarted again, when his victim's heart gave out under the stress. The other two men, perhaps hearing the commotion, fled into the stormy night. Nobody knew whether or not they retrieved their gold. Over the decades, a lot of digging has been done around the old stagecoach depot, though no gold has been found.

ဆ   Only a few miles from Buckhorn, near Crocker, was Wheeler's Mill, the site of two separate stories of lost treasure. The best concerns a couple who operated Wheeler's Mill in 1912 as that essential rural service—flour mill and community store. The husband, in September of that year, died suddenly when he was caught in the belts of some of his equipment. Only a month later, his wife, Agatha, followed his departure, having contracted pneumonia at his funeral.

Shortly before their deaths, Agatha had inherited a substantial amount of money from a relative, but neighbors "turning out" the house after her death, found no resources of any kind, not even enough cash for the funerals. The couple had made wills, leaving everything to relatives and friends, but nothing of value was found. What happened next was reported by Eva Marie Woodward in *Fate* magazine, in the 1950s. She wrote that her young uncle, Clarence Hamilton, worked for the Wheelers after school, on weekends and during vacations. Because they were childless, the couple took affectionate interest in him and he was very fond of them. After their deaths, Clarence was asked to help take inventory of the store.

On the first afternoon after the funeral, coming in as soon as school was out, he was astounded to look up from his work and see Agatha Wheeler

Whoever enjoys not this life,

I count him but an apparition,

though he wear about him

the sensible affections of flesh.

Sir Thomas Browne, "Religio Medici"

standing before him. She was wearing a grey dress he remembered, one with a large white collar and white cuffs. Though she smiled at him in the usual way, he was terrified. Telling the others he was sick, Clarence ran home where he was put to bed and given calming potions.

The next day at the same time, Mrs. Wheeler reappeared to Clarence. This time he was able to stay and work. He just made sure not to look up again. That night his grandmother told Clarence that when ghosts visit us they usually want something. "You should ask Mrs. Wheeler if you can help her," the older woman instructed, "but protect yourself by saying 'In the name of the Father, the Son and the Holy Ghost, what do you want here?'"

When the ghost appeared the next day, Clarence controlled his fear enough to follow his grandmother's instructions. The ghost backed away a few steps and motioned him to follow her. This meant not only crossing the store and the whole mill but also going through a tunnel that led to the house. Once outdoors again, Mrs. Wheeler's image led Clarence to a newly built stone chimney that had been one of her husband's last projects. Making digging motions and pointing down, she left little doubt about what she wanted him to do. Clarence sped home and gathered a crew of reinforcements to help him dig. In only minutes they found a large Dutch oven, carefully sealed and full of gold, currency and investment certificates. Mrs. Wheeler's debts were paid and her loved ones were rewarded as she had intended. No one ever reported seeing her again.

    ℥ The other Wheeler Mill ghost supposedly lost his body there long before Clarence Hamilton's time. He was a victim of bushwhackers (roving renegades that were sometimes former soldiers) soon after the Civil War. The story begins when he stopped in for a night's stay. He was noticeably nervous, and strangely secretive about who he was and where he was from. In the late afternoon, somebody rode in to warn that bushwhackers were in the area. They usually struck mills, which were good sources of supplies and usually harbored a few people who could be robbed. As the mill's owners hurried to hide their inventory and shoppers fled, the strange guest asked to borrow a shovel, took his valise, and ran outside.

When the attack ended, the stranger was among the dead. Belongings in his room gave no clue to his identity. No amount of searching ever revealed what he was so determined to bury. However, it was said he haunted the mill for many years, appearing in the west door when the setting sun impeded vision, as it had on the day of the guerrilla raid. A small man in top hat and frock coat, sometimes seen carrying a bag, he would rush past a spectator and disappear. Occasionally, if the person who had seen him turned quickly, they got a glimpse of him from the back.

How fading are the joys

we dote upon!

Like apparitions

seen and gone.

John Norris, "The Meditation"

Hoax or Haunts?

One of the most audacious ghost stories in history was explored in the *Gateway Guide* for Halloween 1975, when an unidentified writer compiled a series of supposedly genuine newspaper stories from 1940, 1945 and 1974. All three stories involved tales from Fort Leonard Wood. The recap said when soldiers on sentry duty were found drunk and unconscious on Halloween, they all made the same claim: that riotous ghosts—in a language they couldn't understand—had forced them to sip hard cider through a straw until they passed out.

The 1940 article told how residents of Bloodland, a village of about 100 people, learned on Halloween that their homes and town would be sacrificed to the new fort. Gathered for a community celebration when this news was given, the locals were incensed, for their town was an old settlement of home-loving, hard-working German people, many of whom still clung to their native language. The newspaper account said that because many were drinking already, a minor riot took place—one man having to be arrested for trying to raise the Confederate flag in a riotous manner.

Then, in 1942, the *Guide* tells us, a soldier named James Klown (clue here that the reporter was joking?) was court-martialed and confined for a year after being found drunk and unconscious on guard duty. He told his officers that while investigating strange noises in the area, he was taken captive and forced to drink hard cider through a straw until he collapsed. The following year, a soldier named Randall Ellsworth suffered the same fate, but he was not confined and Klown was released. The area was then made off-limits to military personnel. In 1974, however, three men together supposedly told the same tale and the 1975 story ended with the question "What will happen at Fort Leonard Wood tomorrow night?"

Probably all this proves that the more complex and imaginative a ghost story is, the more suspicious we should be. Whoever wrote the story in 1975 is no longer at the *Guide* and nobody now on the staff has any idea whether the whole thing or only part of it was a hoax. This demonstrates how big jokes may be incorporated into folklore, for the ghost story did exist apart from that anonymous newspaper writer, and the writer relayed Bloodland's tragic ending accurately. He gave a moving description of a much-loved little town. Today, having become a firing range, nothing is left, he said, but some foundations and a badly damaged church.

Certainly residents of the doomed town had felt enough outrage and sadness to have possibly stimulated all sorts of supernatural activity. Possibly this supports all those who have speculated that emotion expended in a certain area attracts ghostly manifestations.

Chapter Three

Springfield

Going to college in Springfield exposed me to a new set of ghost stories, some by word of mouth, some from local newspapers, and others from the writings of that famous Ozarks folklorist, Vance Randolph, then at his peak of popularity. Later came other collectors of Ozarks lore, but first, Springfield.

Springfield's most haunted building was probably the Landers Theater. Built in 1907 for live performances, the Landers Theater saw no other use for decades. By the 1920s, as a vaudeville theater, the building was considered to be haunted. As the years passed it did everything a theater can do, being used for showing movies and then for television filming. Its reputation for being haunted persisted even into the 1960s, when the Landers went back to its live-actors roots, as home for the Springfield Little Theater.

The only story remaining as to why the Landers is haunted concerns a despondent stagehand who hanged himself from some of the high rigging above stage. Sources say his body remained there through three performances before his absence—not to mention his body—was noticed. Investigators found no police record of the event, but many records have been lost over the years. All this gentle ghost is reported to do is walk about at times on the

So long as the stories multiply...

and so few are positively explained away,

it is bad method to ignore them.

William James,
American psychologist, in a lecture

catwalks. Only people alone in the empty theater have ever said they've heard him.

Springfield Little Theater's manager, Craig Hutchison, interviewed by Jean Maneke for the Springfield newspaper in the 1970s, seemed unaware of this story. He did say, however, "...this is a hotbed of superstition..." remarking that many theaters are havens for ghost sightings, since their size, big areas of darkness, multiple entrances and exits, and their intricate corridors are suited for real or imitation ghosts.

Hutchison did disprove the rumor that the Landers has secret panels and passages. Having been present through extensive renovation, he knew the walls were nowhere thick enough to allow anything so dramatic. However he conceded that several performers had told him of seeing, from the stage, unsettling sights. Some had said in rehearsal they felt a presence watching from the wings, with intensity and ill will.

The only unusual thing Hutchison had experienced was lights that would not always turn off, even after they were unplugged and the main switch was thrown. He supposed this could have resulted from the building being rewired many times. Nevertheless, whenever it happened, he said he always decided pretty promptly, "Time to be getting home."

Ghosts Affectionate and Otherwise

Another outstanding Springfield manifestation was what a newspaper story called "the hugging ghost." This unexplained entity just seemed to enjoy giving exuberant, prolonged and engulfing hugs that caused at least two people to faint from panic. One recipient who didn't faint said it felt "sort of like being attacked by a mattress."

 ⁖ A Springfield newspaper column called "Over the Ozarks" once printed a letter from Arleen Pomaville of Aurora, which told about a haunted house her great grandparents briefly occupied. It was far from being what one would expect ghosts to like, since the house was just a three-room affair hastily and crudely built to shelter workers. Several identical structures stood in a row, only a few feet between neighbors—yet only the tenants of this one particular little house were constantly leaving, saying it was haunted.

Pomaville's ancestors, being staunch disbelievers in ghosts, moved in. On their very first night, they were awakened by the sharp sound of ripping paper. It seemed to come from overhead and when they lit their lamp, the noise stopped. Thinking it was rats or squirrels they slept with the light on. The next day they climbed up in the shallow attic, but found no indication of animal habitation and no tracks of any kind on the dusty floor.

From ghoulies and ghosties and long-leggety beasties
And things that go bump in the night,
Good Lord, deliver us!

Mark Van Doren, "The Story Teller"

After a few days of peace, the eerie, unexplained paper ripping began again and was joined by a trick of the water bucket. Its dipper took spells of rising and sinking, gurgling loudly all the while. The husband eliminated this problem by simply hanging the dipper on a nail.

The spirit was not to be outdone. Soon came clicking and rattling at the front door, as if someone were trying to jiggle the latch off from outside. This was followed by the back door flying open forcefully, as if someone was angry, or as if blown inward by strong wind. Sometimes both door mysteries and the paper ripping went on simultaneously.

The husband—obviously relishing a challenge—pitted his own strength against the kitchen door. He reported the power behind it was far greater than his own. When pushing the sturdy kitchen table against the door didn't help, he nailed a thick leather strap across it, anchored strongly on each side. The haunted door snapped even the thick leather, so the couple admitted defeat and moved away. They conceded to neighbors that they'd been losing too much sleep, not that they'd ever been frightened.

The Phantom Flivver

College students warned each other that in the Nixa area one must beware of a brand-new-looking Model A Ford, which day or night, but mostly night, might suddenly appear and cause a wreck. A sheriff named Frank Jones had died in 1932, belief was, by being forced off the road by "the phantom flivver." (This word was popular slang in the 1920s for an automobile of little quality or value.) A well-known businessman, Fred McCoy, said he almost wrecked his car to avoid hitting the fabled Ford.

So long as another vehicle was in sight, drivers were safe. But on the Ozarks' seldom used and winding roads drivers were often alone. The silent appearance of round, but dim headlights could mean danger. Some people declared that the ghostly car's horn issued a derisive "Ahooooooooga" salute as it departed. Nobody ever said they heard an engine.

No explanation existed as to why the phantom car patrolled the area. Vance Randolph, in his book *Ozark Magic and Folklore*, said the dangerous car was taken quite seriously by people in the area. Many claimed they had seen it. Some said they damaged their own vehicles because of the Model A.

The Sheedy Farm

A suicide, two grisly murders, a fearsome albino protector, seven siblings who never left their parents, a showplace farm allowed to fall into decay: all of these are elements of the story told about a pre-Civil War estate near Springfield. The place was first known as Springlawn and was so

What? And did the thing

appear again tonight?

Shakespeare, "Hamlet"

idyllic that people drove out from town on Sundays to view its beautiful house, many farm buildings, lakes, waterfall and deer park. One of Springlawn's great attractions was its herd of lovely Jersey cattle.

After several years, owner Frank Headley sold the farm to Mike Sheedy, his wife, and their seven children. The Sheedys all lived out their lives there, the last sister dying in 1979. The final years of the farm saw the property fall into pitiful disrepair as the three women alone tried to keep it up. It took on the appearance of the standard haunted house, in ruin, almost consumed by vines and shrubs completely gone amuck. Some writers say the three sisters hired a large albino man to help them, but that he grew so possessive he turned away visitors at gunpoint. He also was blamed for two hatchet murders done at a nearby little iron bridge, one of which was a decapitation—the weapon defiantly left at the scene.

According to Tom Mason, writing in *Springfield!* magazine in October 1985, the bridge began to be called Hatchet Man's Bridge and the farm, Albino Farm. One of the Sheedy sons' having killed himself there added to the eerie atmosphere of the place and assured its being considered haunted. Mason did not give details of that, but when the house burned in 1988, its legend remained. At the time he wrote his article, stone pillars still stood at the entrance and many people drove north on Farm Road 165 to see them and talk about the tragedies there, just as people had driven out a century earlier to see a farm so beautiful and productive it could hardly be believed.

Neighboring Ghosts

Springfield papers also carried ghost stories from nearby towns. One story from Ozark centered around a house that was built of boards taken from a scaffold on which bandits had been hanged. Locals said that when the house was new, fluttering and popping sounds coincided with the time of day when the prisoners had met their fate. These stopped at 3 p.m., the hour at which the execution was completed. Ten years to the day and hour of execution, a clock in that house, a clock that hadn't run for years, began on its own accord and ran through 3 p.m. at which time it stopped and could never be made to go again.

Meanwhile, a neighbor had an experience she felt was connected. While working outdoors, she was approached by a perfectly real looking young man who asked her about someone who'd hanged himself from a nearby bridge. As she explained that she knew nothing about this, the young man disappeared before her eyes.

Chapter Four

The Ozarks

No collector of Ozarks folklore compares to Vance Randolph, who dedicated about 50 years of his life to the task of compiling Ozarks folklore. His books are still sought after and used as reference. His ghost stories range from only a few sentences, to tales long and detailed, with full credit given to all those he quoted.

Randolph, the "dean of American folklorists," often referred to a collector who went before him, Thomas Moore of Ozark. In 1938 Moore, an attorney by profession, had published a book called *Mysterious Tales and Legends of the Ozarks*. It's interesting to compare Moore's book with *Ozark Magic and Folklore*, one of Randolph's most popular works, first published in 1947 as *Ozarks Superstitions*. Here's an example of why it's fun to compare both men's work.

Randolph wrote of a Taney County farmer who insisted that his deceased daughter was still singing in the woods in late afternoon as had been her custom in life. When derided for saying this, he invited some solid citizens, including a judge and a few attorneys, out to listen. Some of the men said yes, they heard a female voice singing, clearly enough to almost

make out words. One said several lines ended in yodeling. Everyone agreed that they had heard something. One witness questioned by Randolph years later, said he'd not swear he heard a human voice, but that there was something pleasant and melodic, unlike any birdsong or other natural sound he'd ever heard. He said the men walked together through the woods where the singer seemed to be, coming toward them, then veering away again. They found no tracks, no crushed vegetation or bruised leaves in the heavily wooded area.

Moore's version of this tale, several pages long, describes this event "in the bend of Finley Creek." He said the girl's name was Madelaine, and that she had died soon after her father had turned her away in bad weather. She had come to him on foot, her baby in her arms, seeking refuge from a failed marriage. Having forbidden the alliance in the first place, he told her she must lie in the bed she'd made and rear her own child. Though other relatives took Madelaine and her baby in, she became ill, possibly from exposure forced by her father, and died.

The whole time, Madelaine's mother had wanted to take her back, and their community also let the father feel its disapproval. So perhaps he had good motivation for choosing to believe the girl was now showing her forgiveness—alive in spirit and still singing, happy near her childhood home. A debunker would probably say her father almost certainly arranged to have someone sing in the woods for witnesses, though of course, even if they all believed it was Madelaine, that would hardly restore his reputation.

For a long time, people visited the site and gave varied reports of what they heard. Some who had known Madelaine declared that they recognized her voice. Others, present with these believers, said they heard nothing at all. As in many ghost stories, opposing perceptions are typical.

The Smiling Spook

Some of Randolph's tales came from groups who shared experiences. The most inexplicable happened in a deserted schoolhouse named Oak Grove, 50 miles south of Springfield. An actual bushwhacker victim, homeless and mentally afflicted, who had sheltered in the school, was said to haunt the building. Supposedly, he appeared as a bald man grinning at spectators from inside a window.

A group of four or more young men, enroute home from a dance and possibly well-liquored, decided to test this story out and sure enough, saw the "h'ant" sitting at the window. When their civil greetings got no response, one fired six times through the glass. The unknown target sat without moving, his expression unchanged. The two bravest boys went inside and came out saying nobody was in the one-room building. Their companions swore

My spectre around me

night and day

Like a wild beast

guards my way.

William Blake, "Poems from Mms"

that the bald man grinned crazily at them the entire time their friends were gone. They then took their own turn going inside but found the same emptiness. More shooting may have taken place at this time. The experiment ended when their horses decided they had reached saturation point for strange doings and bolted for home.

Some Randolph Short Shorts

Travelers near Rogersville saw, from a little distance, a cabin with smoke from its chimney and agreed to stop there for much-needed refreshment. When they reached it, they found the building unoccupied, with no sign of a fire having been on the hearth for years.

      🙰   Near Miney, a correspondent of Randolph's named Mary Elizabeth Mahnkey told him of sighting, through field glasses, a pleasant ridgetop cabin with all signs of habitation. When she inquired about it, she was told by longtime residents of the area that no such cabin existed or ever had.

      🙰   An elderly lady in McDonald County told Randolph of an evening when she sat alone, as usual, in her two-room cabin, doors and windows securely locked against the night. She heard the latch and bolt of the kitchen door lift, and a heavy man in squeaky boots cross to the water bucket. The rattling dipper meant he was getting a drink, and before he could have walked back out, she was in the kitchen. She found nobody there and all entrances were fastened from the inside, just as she had left them.

      🙰   On her deathbed, a young woman distantly related to Randolph, tried to tell her family the name of the man whose betrayal caused her death. Unable to make them understand, she was believed to have come back as the ghost who began walking that house at night, opening and closing drawers of an old bureau. Did they hold evidence of her cruel lover's identity which she hoped she was leading her family to? Randolph didn't speculate.

      🙰   A couple of headless ghosts were listed by Randolph. One haunted the area around a bridge near Kimberling City, gliding about as if on roller skates, or sometimes lying beside the road on very cold nights, groaning horribly. The other was sometimes seen sitting on top of haystacks and would wave at people and then slide down the other side. Nothing was ever there, of course, if anyone went around and looked.

. . . the supernatural, I suspect,

resembles nature in that,

though you drive it out with a pitchfork,

it always comes creeping back . . .

D. J. Enright, editor, "The Oxford Book of Death"

Breadtray Mountain

Sobs, groans and screams from a spot on Breadtray Mountain, a unique formation in Stone County, were explained by Randolph as Spanish soldiers being annihilated by Indians or vice versa. Between the reports of Randolph and Moore we get varied possibilities. Chickasaw tribesmen had mined silver and crafted it on the mountain for generations. Then Spanish explorers came along and imprisoned them in their mine, forcing them to work on as slaves, until the Indians revolted and killed their captors.

Another version is that when the Spaniards arrived, the Indians greeted them generously, helped them find all they needed for their camp and even provided some young women to do the drudgery. When the Indians discovered their daughters and sisters were being abused, they wiped out the newcomers. Some authors have written that these sounds were later heard by people in groups, all of whom made similar reports.

The late Tom Ladwig, a *Columbia Tribune* columnist, added to this story by more precisely locating the mountain which is now partly inundated by Table Rock Lake, about ten miles from Reed Springs, near the northern border of Arkansas. He said that a great deal of searching for the Chickasaw/Spanish treasure had taken place in the area and he ended with characteristic humor, warning whoever might get close to the silver that "a great white Internal Revenue Service Man is probably there and watching."

A Truly Complex Tale

One of Moore's longer stories was about a rotting mansion somewhere in southern Missouri. People heard footsteps start on the porch and move down the hall and into a large room with a beautiful fireplace, where they paused for some time, before departing in a deliberate manner. Inhabitants of this home also heard the weak cry of an infant near the back door, and an untraceable creaky chair in which someone seemed to be rocking vigorously. Finally, some roses on this property once took on an odor enticingly like bananas and lured a small boy almost to his death.

The history of this house, pieced together by two sets of owners, their relatives, and people who worked there as servants was this: A Georgian who happened to be an abolitionist, came north with his wife and servants and in 1847 built a lovely home. When the Civil War began, he felt compelled to go, and with strangely thoughtless haste. He sent his wife back to her parents with some of the most capable and trusted slaves, taking only one wagonload of possessions. He asked the slaves who were left behind to care for the place and the valuables within it as well as they could, and live

Then shall the dust return

to the earth as it was:

and the spirit shall return

unto God who gave it.

The Bible, Ecclestiastes

on its livestock and produce. After the war, which he assured them would be short, they would all reassemble and see what they should do. He had long ago promised freedom to his slaves, as soon as he could arrange for them to go out into the world well equipped to take care of themselves.

After his wife departed, the owner of the mansion sent his servant to bring up their two horses. While waiting, he reentered the house, and stood for a few moments in contemplation before a large portrait of his wife that hung over the mantel in the parlor. Then he went back outside, mounted his horse, and rode off with his attendant.

The Georgian was killed by Confederates at Pea Ridge within weeks of his enlistment. When his wife learned of it some months later she died of grief and shock. According to their will, their property went to relatives from Georgia, but the war prevented these people from taking possession. Meanwhile, the house was ravaged by a succession of guerrilla and military groups who needed shelter. Surprisingly, it was never totally destroyed. Most of the slaves remained, since they had nowhere else to go and most felt loyalty and affection for the departed owner.

At least one tragedy occurred during the numerous military occupations of the house. A slave with a young baby was clubbed to death at the back of the house for breaking a curfew the intruders had imposed. No one dared to go out and get the baby, which lay in its dead mother's arms until it died of hunger and exposure.

The creaky rocking chair, one of the hauntings that most disturbed the relatives who eventually claimed their inheritance, was never explained. Soon the new occupants were all sleeping in one room together—their dog included. They practically gave the house away in order to raise enough money to move to a much more humble and more wholesome place. They warned the buyer that the place was haunted, but he was unconcerned.

Apparently this family, which included two rowdy little boys, was not much disturbed by the ghosts. They first thought the rocking chair was branches rubbing against the house or a loose eave trough moving in the wind. Careful attention to these possibilities didn't stop the sounds. The mother went to the back door hundreds of times, just in case the crying she heard was a real baby someone had abandoned. When she had tea parties in the parlor and footsteps came into the room, she would laugh and tell her guests, "That's just our ghost. He never hurts anyone." Sometimes she would demonstrate what her children had discovered: if one stood in the path of the steps, they paused for a moment, but then just continued on the other side of the living barrier.

The banana episode made this family take the haunts more seriously. The boy said the delicious odor came from a particularly lovely big rose

True love is like ghosts,

which everybody talks about

and few have seen.

François, Duc de la Rochefoucauld

thought to have been brought from Alabama by the original owners. Bananas being uncommon in that time and place, and much coveted by children, he happily devoured several roses. His resulting desperate illness was barely remedied by a combination of doctor and home efforts. The bush was never reported to smell of bananas again, and Moore did not tell us what became of the brave family or of the house.

Steele's Spin on Ozark Ghosts

Phillip Steele of Springdale, Arkansas wrote several books about historical events and notable people of the Ozarks and has produced two videos about the haunted areas. Though most of what he covers is in his home state, the videos (available from Ozark Mountaineer Book Store) will interest ghost buffs and do contain some Missouri material.

One of the most interesting stories in Steele's book *Ozarks Tales and Superstitions* is about the ghost of something that never was alive, a locomotive's caboose. In the 1930s a number of respected people in Arkansas and Missouri reported seeing this caboose moving serenely over the tracks all by itself. No explanatory story existed, apparently.

Another Steele story is one of those about an Indian maiden who kills herself because she cannot marry the man she loves, but his has an unusually significant twist. In this case, the girl was named Moon Song, and the man was a Spaniard. Her father forbade their union, almost succeeded in killing the suitor and was going to force his daughter to marry a man of his own choosing. Unable to accept this indignity, she threw herself off of a cliff that rises more than 300 feet above the James River in southern Missouri. Her remorseful father had his medicine man put a curse on the area, to repel anything that might disturb the peace of Moon Song's spirit.

Accordingly, when white men came, with their determination to utilize all they could for profit, they found some opposition. A strange turbulence existed near the cliff where, unknown to them, Moon Song's body had entered the water. Boats entering the eddy were likely to capsize and many fishermen and explorers died at what came to be called Virgin Shoal or the Virgin's Swirl. Up on the cliff, hunters had strange accidents, often fatal. Efforts to integrate this ideal bluff into a dam had to be abandoned because so many things went wrong. There were fires, equipment failures, extremes of weather, and accidents to workers. As the Moon Song story became known, problems were even greater. Workers tended to leave suddenly, declaring they had heard a woman's inconsolable weeping. Nobody could convince them it was only the wind blowing through lacy crevices in the eroding cliff. Finally, Moon Song's spirit was left in peace.

…are we so advanced

in our knowledge

that we can prove

the impossibility of ghosts?

Gotthold Ephraim Lessing,
"Hamburgische Dramaturgie"

Steele commented that to this day the curse is blamed for upsetting cameras. Many tourists complain about disappointing results on what they thought would make wonderful pictures, with light being perfect, and automatic exposure and focus leaving little to chance. Perhaps some day Wind Song's spirit will rejoin that of her lover, and superb pictures can once again be taken of the beauties of the Breadtray Mountains.

Stories from Students

In the 1960s an English teacher named Ellen Massey (now a well-known member of the Missouri Writers' Hall of Fame) led her Lebanon High School students in a class called Ozarkia, to collect lore of the area. From their work came a magazine named *Bittersweet* which critics have compared favorably with the *Foxfire* series. Several times they collected ghost stories, and here are three of their best, used in *The Old Settler's Gazette*, published annually in Dixon as part of its historical celebration.

෩   Travelers who camped near a certain deserted mill were routinely awakened by the sounds of wood chopping in a nearby grove. The constant sounds destroyed their sleep, both chopping and occasional pauses for sharpening the axe on a grindstone. Randolph wrote of this too, saying it was reported from several places in the Ozarks.

෩   Near Houston lived a farm couple who were expecting a baby, in days long before going to hospitals for birthing was routine. When the time came, the father-to-be set out on horseback with a friend to get a doctor. They had not gone far down the road before they encountered a woman dressed in white, walking, a baby in her arms. "We must go back," the husband said. "My wife is dead." He was right. Back home, his wife's mother told him the hour of death, which coincided with the ghostly appearance.

෩   A mother working in her garden, or in the fields, had put her baby out to play on a quilt nearby. Among its toys was a rattle which it shook with particular vigor. The mother was glad, for as long as she heard the rattle, she needn't stop to see about the child. However, when the baby began laughing wildly and continued to do so without pausing, she went over and to her horror, she found her child clutching and shaking a rattlesnake. She ran for her tools, and with one blow decapitated the reptile. It had not bitten the baby, but in only a few weeks the child sickened and died. The outcome is predictable: the sound of a baby's rattle, perhaps blended with the sound of a snake's rattlers, can still be heard in the grass where the snake who did *not* bite the baby was beheaded by a terrified mother.

Chapter Five

Columbia &
Boone County

ocated in the heart of Missouri, Columbia surely has the state's highest concentration of romantic ghost stories. There are the lovers of Senior Hall at Stephens College, the lovelorn grey lady at Christian College, the unhappy bride of Hathman House and the home-loving ghost at Sutton Place who may have had a bit of a crush on her flesh-and-blood housemate. Probably we shouldn't be surprised at any of this, since the area has teemed with young people for many generations. Often called "College Town USA," Columbia is home to three colleges. Stephens College was founded in 1833, the University of Missouri in 1839, and Christian College in 1851.

Though the Senior Hall story seems far removed from truth, if it indeed has any basis in fact, it's too good to dismiss. Supposedly an Independence girl named Sarah Jane Wheeler was a senior in 1862 and living in one of the oldest buildings on campus, then a residence hall. Somehow, she became involved with a Confederate corporal named Isaac Johnson. According to the version one chooses, Isaac had either escaped from federal forces then occupying Columbia and climbed through her window in a desperate search for refuge, or he had deserted his post elsewhere and sought

I long to talk with some old lover's ghost…

John Donne, "Love's Deity"

her out because of a previous relationship. A third version even tells that Isaac came to Columbia to assassinate General Henry Halleck, commander of the Union soldiers. This would have avenged his father, killed by Grant's army in the South. Some stories indicate it was not Sarah he was seeking but her roommate, Margaret Parker, of Little Rock, Arkansas.

At any rate, the girls took pity on the exhausted and famished soldier, and kept him hidden for several days. Margaret's family had sent two slaves to school with her, their working for the school to constitute her tuition, and she was thus able to command help in getting food for Isaac and taking care of his other needs.

According to *Haunted Heartland*, by Beth Scott and Michael Norman, Sarah and Isaac fell in love during this short acquaintance. His presence was inevitably discovered, and Halleck, alert for problems among Confederate sympathizers, quickly arrested Isaac. The book says he had the young man executed by firing squad under Sarah's window, as an object lesson to other girls who might befriend the enemy, and that Yankees tolled the bell in Senior Hall's tower to emphasize the event. Sarah then rushed up into the tower and threw herself out, or hung herself from the bell's ropes.

Unfortunately for the story's credibility, Columbia historian John Crighton wrote that Senior Hall had no bell tower in 1862, that it was not added for at least a decade. That does no damage to other endings for the story that include the lovers escaping the college only to drown together in the flooded Hinkson Creek or the Missouri River. Alan Havig, professor of American History at Stephens College and author of a book of Columbia history, confirms Crighton's information and says college archives offer nothing on any of these events.

Nonetheless, students cling to the fun of believing that Sarah may walk the halls of a building recently restored to much the appearance it would have had when she lived there. At Halloween they sometimes pay her the compliment of a vigil, and at least once a team of psychical investigators was scheduled to visit Senior Hall to analyze what one student termed "the unusualness" there. These investigators said that inhabiting spirits should be warned that huge changes would soon be made to their abode, with increased human activity to follow. Results were not reported by the papers. Perhaps the visit never materialized. Senior Hall now is used for recitals and music and dance classes, as well as for conferences and other meetings.

Christian's Grey Lady

When the Grey Lady began to walk at Christian College, it was not the coeducational school it is today, now renamed Columbia College. Back then its all-female enrollment included many southern belles, since

Your ghost will walk,

You lover of trees

(If our loves remain),

In an English lane.

Robert Browning, "De Gustibus"

Boone County was settled mainly by people from the states of Kentucky, Tennessee and Virginia. One of these girls, whose name now seems to be lost to time, was engaged to a young man serving in the Confederate army. She vowed to wear only grey clothing so long as he did, and until she could put on her white wedding gown.

When her fiancé was killed by Union soldiers in Columbia, not far from the college, the girl immediately jumped from a three-story building called the Conservatory, which is now known as Williams Hall. As a spirit, she manifested herself mainly as a fleeting figure in grey, usually glimpsed on overcast, foggy or misty days, which left people hardly certain of who or what they had seen. Sometimes she also seemed to pass through college buildings at certain times of day, creating an almost indescribable presence, which some people felt strongly and some not at all.

This spirit had her benevolent side: sometimes, it's said, students returned to their rooms to find their ironing done. On days that became unexpectedly hot, windows might be thoughtfully raised to let in fresh air. An interesting little note on the haunting at Christian College just on a basis of her attire: "grey lady" is a term used in literature of the paranormal for ghosts of women who died violently for the sake of love.

In 1965 Christian's grey lady did a striking encore, gliding sedately past windows on the third floor of St. Clair Hall, a building which did not exist while she lived. Carrying a candle, she seemingly passed through walls, for all rooms opened onto a hallway running parallel to the windows and her progress was uninterrupted. Students out in a group, serenading, were amazed to see, on St. Clair's top floor, a white figure with a light slowly moving past the windows of vacant dormitory rooms. A few courageous girls rushed into the building, and though they found nothing there, it was only a few days before everyone knew that Penny Pitman, one of Christian's most admired and gifted students, had been "campused," or confined to school grounds, for the hoax, along with a fellow prankster from Texas.

Dean Elizabeth Kirkman, whose office was in a tower of St. Clair, happened to be at work that night and well remembers the excitement of the girls who burst in on her to report "a light on the top floor, going right through the walls!"

"They were very frightened, or pretended to be," she says. Only one clue, never revealed to Pitman, told the dean immediately who to send for. Penny Pitman was, she says, "a brilliant student, winner of a trustee's scholarship...active in athletics and many campus activities, very popular with the other girls, but mischievious...mischievious." The dean adds, "I asked her, 'Penny, what are you trying to do? Scare everyone to death?' She grinned and said, 'I guess so.'"

He was eaten of worms

and gave up the ghost.

The Bible, Acts

Interview with a Ghost

Pitman, who now lives in St. Charles and restores houses, was not at all adverse to sharing how she and her friend achieved their puzzling effect. While one of them walked across one room, the other, identically clad in a big beach towel, waited on the other side of the connecting wall, candle concealed, until her partner knocked to let her know that her own walk should begin. Then the first ghost scurried out into the hall and past the room being haunted, into the next room, and waited for the signal, ready to walk in her turn while the other scurried. Thus they made their giggling, breathless way across the top floor of a building they knew a group of other students would be passing that night. In the dark, their candles attracted eyes of the passersby, just as they'd hoped.

It had been fun, Pitman says, checking out the upstairs earlier and deciding just how to do their reenactment. "I don't think we had to find keys to get up there," she says. "There was no reason for anyone to go; it was just empty rooms. Staircases went down at each end of the hall, so we were sure we could get out quickly if we needed to."

Being confined to campus was not, to Pitman and her friend, a big price to pay for the fun they'd had. The college yearbook, *The Ivy Chain*, that year used a Grey Lady theme, with illustrations portraying a ghost whose swirling gown revealed jeans and sandals.

A Sad Bride

Now for the story of the sad bride of Haden House. This story starts when Joel Harris Haden came to Boone County in 1828 at the age of 17. W. M. Switzer, in his book on the history of Boone County, called Haden "one of the county's most successful citizens."

By the time he was 20, Haden had a fine farm and house and returned south to take a wife. She was Sarah Cave, 17, very pretty, but not robust. Perhaps she had some health problem, or had been too pampered at home, or was just too young for the responsibilities of wifehood at the time. Maybe she could not accept the loss of close contact with her family and lifelong friends. In any case, after a few years that seem to have been less than happy, she died, a victim of the typhoid epidemic of 1835. The historical part of the story does not indicate whether Haden brought another wife to his farm, or whether anything especially unpleasant had happened to Sarah there. The contemporary part of the story is that Jack Crouch, who occupied the Haden House with his wife in the early 1980s, told local newspapers he twice awakened to find a woman standing in his bedroom door. The first time she looked perfectly real and substantial; the second time

There are no ghosts around here, Jeffy.
They have their own towns.

Bill Kean's cartoon, "Family Circus"

there was a haziness about her. These experiences—and others, which convinced him that the place was haunted—did not stop him from converting it, in 1984, to a restaurant that became one of the most prestigious in the Columbia area.

No unusual experience for customers is on record, but many employees, half-afraid, half-amused, blamed Sarah that Haden House had an unusual number of dish breakages, equipment mishaps, and electrical problems. A number of bizarre and inexplicable things happened, such as the turntable on a gearless phonograph that was prone to spinning madly. In another incident, members of a band performing at the Haden House on a regular basis left their expensive, elaborate sound equipment stored there, carefully secured, carefully adjusted just as it needed to be while not in use. Nobody but themselves had access to the storage area. One day they came in to find things in crazy disarray, hardly a switch and knob as they had left it. Haden House closed as a restaurant in 1988 and was standing vacant when this was written.

The House a Ghost Loved

I n January 1988, *Fate Magazine* published, with cooperation of a practicing psychologist named Fred Nolen, a story that is hard to dismiss as hoax or illusion. Several people went on record in print or on television with supporting experience. Nolan said he lived for several years with an affectionate ghost who shared his interest in music and his love for a condemned farmhouse near the edge of Columbia. Before the *Fate Magazine* article, he described his life there for television station KOMU and the *Columbia Missourian*. Others were quoted in the magazine and elsewhere.

Nolen was renting a big old place known as the Sutton House. It had once been a fine farm house, property of a prominent Boone County family, but "development" doomed its swelling fields, its woods and lovely little lake to oblivion. Giant trees and some determined flowers, still blooming in obedience to planters long dead, would all be bulldozed. This saddened Nolen, and perhaps intensified his enjoyment of the beauty around him. With books, piano, pets and many guests, his was a simple, relaxed life in the deteriorating house. Though other changes went forward in the area, for some reason, destruction of the house itself was repeatedly postponed. Nolen had spent years there before anything unusual happened.

The otherworldly activity began with what Nolen termed "the classic haunted house things." He heard jingling chains, a light pounding, small objects rolling about on the attic floor. Sometimes mobiles or tablecloths moved when there were no indoor drafts. Though never indicating fear, his pets often seemed to be looking at things he could not see.

During daylight,

they listen with approval

when ghosts are ridiculed,

but in the dead of night they shudder

as they listen to tales about them.

Gotthold Ephraim Lessing,
"Hamburgische Dramaturgie"

Gradually, Nolen began to feel someone beside him at times. This came to happen always when he stood looking out and thinking of how much he liked the house and its surroundings; he felt someone else was sharing his pleasure. Soon tactile feelings began. It might be a light, friendly hand on his shoulder as he played the piano—or, for *In the Mood*, with its rumbling bass chords, a playful ruffle of the hair on the back of his neck.

At last Nolen saw his companion briefly while in a state of sleep paralysis. He said she floated by his bed, apparently unaware of him. She was a small, fine-featured young woman with long brown hair parted in the center, falling straight on each side. She wore a long, simple grey robe, and "drifted through the closed door," Nolen said. "I never saw her again."

A few of Nolen's visitors also saw this apparition. One woman, driving up to his house, glimpsed a girl in an upstairs window. Nolen was not at home, she knew, his motorcycle being gone, so the visitor assumed she'd seen a house guest. Going inside, she called out. Getting no response, she looked through every room and didn't find anyone there. Later she described to Nolen the very same ghostly girl he had seen.

Another friend, Julie, holder of a Ph.D., a serious student of the paranormal, gave a fuller description. She said she met the ghost in the kitchen. Appearance was much the same, but the person's old-fashioned dress was not completely buttoned up and her hair was disordered, as if she'd just arisen and was looking for the day's first cup of coffee. Seemingly startled at the psychic's presence, she backed away through the closed door. Later, Julie says she was talking with Nolen in the kitchen, and the entity appeared in the doorway, then withdrew quietly, exactly like a person who has inadvertently intruded on private conversation. Nolen saw nothing then, for his back was to the door.

Once Nolen heard his housemate sing, however. He said her voice was "crystal pure...like a heavenly flute," wordlessly repeating the tune he had just played. Another time, two female guests heard her. They were in separate rooms and each thought the other was singing. Others present heard nothing.

Researching the history of the Sutton House, Nolen learned that two women had hanged themselves on the property, one in the barn in 1856 and one from a tree in 1940. He felt sure that his spirit companion was neither of them, but someone untroubled, perhaps a frequent guest who'd formed an attachment for the place in happy circumstances. He believed she reached out to him because he shared her affection for the house.

When asked if he wasn't afraid of his ghost, Nolen said, "She's a lot less dangerous than people can be." Julie termed her "totally harmless...a gentle soul, a drifting person." When Nolan finally had to leave, as the site

May it not be that someday

from this dream of time

This chronicle of smoke,

this strange and bitter miracle of life,

In which we are the moving

and phantasmal figures,

We shall awake?

Thomas Wolfe, quoted by Alan J. Smith

was slated for a new housing development, he was asked what he thought the ghost would do once the house was gone. He speculated that she might harass the contractors. Or she might go with the staircase, which she especially seemed to love. He was sure someone would salvage that graceful piece of work. Nolen said he'd invited the spirit to follow him, but never felt her presence in his new home, though he played all the songs she liked. His last word was that maybe she was somehow securely in the past. Maybe she would have the house for all time no matter what was done to it.

A Few Unromantic Ghosts

Columbia Missourian newspaper stories written for Halloween in 1990 and 1992, said three university fraternities claim their houses are haunted.

Sigma Phi Epsilon members say their third floor has been haunted by a young woman who lived there when a sorority owned the house in the 1940s. She was Jewish, from Europe and, on learning that her parents had died in a concentration camp, is said to have hanged herself by fastening a rope to a radiator and jumping from a window.

A floating reddish light and footsteps on the stairs and hallway have been features of this haunting, but Tom Schuman, who used the room for a year, said he had "a roommate" who once awakened him with loud feminine giggling close at hand. Nobody could be seen in the hallway or street outside. Another member, Steve Petisto, who spent Christmas vacation of 1987 in the house, says he locked things properly when he went out, and turned off all lights, but on returning would find doors open, lights blazing, and showers running full blast.

In another Greek house, Delta Sigma Phi members say they have seen the apparition of a petite young woman with "flat, black hair" forming a flapper's curl on each cheek and wearing 1920s era pajamas. They think she was a girl named Eleanor who died there of appendicitis when a sorority owned the house. One member, Brent Guglielmino said he believes he saw Eleanor in the basement once, "...just kind of hovering there, back in the corner." The girl stared at him blankly and then floated from the room.

Oddities in the house included flickering lights and televisions, and footsteps and slamming doors, but residents also saw some poltergeist-like activity. Socks flew, they said, and hats fell from racks. Travis Wims said his electric alarm once woke him as usual, when power to the house was off.

Sigma Alpha Epsilon members believe their disturbances rise from the basement which was dug for a house on their site that burned in 1907. This house had sheltered mental patients and had served as a morgue for Civil War casualties. At one time fraternity members thought "Bloody" Bill Anderson was among them and certainly one might expect devilment from

*True science will not deny
the existence of things
because they cannot be weighed
and measured…if a phenomenom does exist,
it demands some kind of explanation.*

Sir Stanley Jevons, "The Principle of Science"

his spirit if spirits have options. The facts on Anderson, however, are that he died in Ray County near Albany, and was buried in Richmond, Missouri, after his body had been displayed contemptuously for a day or two.

Even so, the chapter's tradition is that Confederate soldiers are sometimes seen in their basement and that in 1947, when a pledge class was forced to spend a night there, the boys all de-pledged the next day and would never explain why. Steve Strauss, a 1989 graduate, says he saw a soldier and "You have to respect a situation that scares so many people...so many have lived here...so much has happened here...it seems inevitable that, if there are spirits...they'd come back to visit."

A Threatening Encounter

The *Columbia Missourian* newspaper article for Halloween 1994 offered an experience of Floyd Strader, a Columbian whose hobby is documenting old cemeteries, a service much appreciated by genealogists and other researchers as well as by historical societies. He makes lists of names and dates that are in danger of being lost forever, data that often takes hard work and ingenuity to decipher on the oldest of headstones.

Though one might expect a ghostly happening or two for someone who spends so much time alone in isolated little graveyards, Strader said he only once met anything hostile, and that was not directly. It came on a day when he took his wife and two sons along on a jaunt that included the Maupin Cemetery near Columbia. The afternoon was very hot, but when he returned to his family, they were all in the car, windows rolled up tight and doors locked, quite upset. They said somebody or something they couldn't see had circled the car, beating on the sides and top and had bounced the whole vehicle up and down several times. They told him emphatically they would never again go with him to that cemetery.

Photographs Strader took that day were fine in every cemetery but Maupin; stones he'd photographed there had so many obstructing lines across them that he had to go back later and reshoot. He commented, in talking about this many years later, that as the crow flies, Maupin Cemetery is quite close to Confederate Hill, a Boone County house that is said to be haunted by the spirits of Civil War soldiers and runaway slaves.

And a Reassuring One

Elaine Kline of Columbia tells of a confirming contact she had from a very close friend, Robin, who had just died. The Klines, in St. Louis for the funeral, were staying in the apartment Robin had shared with her husband, also recently deceased. Both women had been active in groups study-

Oh, who would not leave the flesh

to become a reliable spirit,

Possibly traveling far and acquiring merit?

Stevie Smith,
"Longing for Death Because of Feebleness"

ing the paranormal and Robin had often said that after she passed over, she'd get in touch, if that proved to be possible.

Accordingly, Elaine watched for a sign, and when lights began going off and on, said to her husband, "That could be Robin." An electrical engineer, he assured Elaine there are many reasons for power fluctuations. While he searched the apartment for something out of order and looked for the fuse box, Elaine, alone in the living room, was visited by Robin.

"It was not full body," she says. "Her legs and feet were not visible, but I could see she was wearing a lavender dress. There was some haziness to some of the figure, but her face and smile were very clear." Though the apparition said nothing, her expression and, Elaine thinks, some ESP, said clearly, "What did I tell you?" Then she was gone, but she had effectively reinforced positive convictions the two friends held about the hereafter.

Ashland's Ghost Hunter

Until recently, near Ashland, lived a man named Russ Hawkins, who had a lively interest in the supernatural as well as in folklore and tall tales. He seems the epitome of someone R.P. Shelley wrote of in "Hymn to Intellectual Beauty:"

> *...I sought for ghosts, and sped*
> *Through many a listening chamber, cave and ruin,*
> *And starlight wood, with fearful steps pursuing*
> *Hopes of high talk with the departed dead.*

For Hawkins made a point of visiting a number of places reputed to be haunted and he studied such matters enough that his opinion and experience were often consulted by others. Unfortunately, Hawkins seems to have written none of this down, but several friends remember his stories. One was small and simple, but has the power to raise one's hair a little.

Hawkins told of being at work in a huge hayfield in summer's blistering heat and being only one of several workers who could see, almost out of sight across the rolling terrain, another team of men working with hay wagons and horses. His group didn't know what to think, since they had understood the whole job of cutting this field was theirs—enough work for two or three days.

After one of the youngest, most energetic workers walked toward the other team, shouting and getting no response, the men told themselves it was a mirage, or that they were all getting too dry and close to sunstroke. They drank a lot more water and lemonade, resumed work and saw the ghostly team no more, until they were starting in with their loaded wagons.

A subtle spirit has my path attended

In likeness not a lion but a pard;

And when the arrows flew like hail and hard,

He licked my wounds,

and all my wounds were mended.

Elinor Wylie, "Address to my Soul"

Then they looked across the field and saw that the others, too, were pulling out. The field itself soon hid them from sight, but no unfamiliar wagons joined Hawkins' group at the barn. Their employer assured them nobody else was cutting for him and sent them out next morning to finish up. This included getting in the untouched hay their counterparts had worked so hard on the day before.

Anyone who has spent many days in hayfields might remark that the possibility of being sentenced to an eternity of fruitlessly doing that work, would be a good deterrent for any crime!

Hawkins had a better story than this, though. Some say he told it as his own experience, some as another's. But someone on a horse or bicycle trip needed water or something else and being in a sparsely settled area, stopped at an unpromising house. It hardly looked inhabited, but peering in the windows he decided it was, though nobody came to the door. Going around to the back, he found a frail old man in pitiful clothing sitting on a well platform. The man's poor color suggested the worst of health, but he was friendly and interested in the traveler's problems.

As they talked, he asked if the traveler had seen a newspaper lately. "This morning," was the reply, and the old man asked, "Well, what did it say about Sherman? How far has he got? Does it look like the old coot will really be able to split the South and give it to Lincoln for Christmas?"

Alarmed at what this seemed to say about the mental condition of the person before him, the traveler looked down for an instant to compose the best answer, and raised his eyes to find himself alone. The area was too large for anyone to have got out of sight so quickly, even at the peak of health. Hawkins considered this a bona fide meeting with a ghost.

One Last Story

One last Boone County story took place not long ago at Wildwood Farm, a training and teaching horse facility operated by Terry and Lynn Frazee. Lynn says, "I grew up in a haunted house," referring to Skyrim Farm, property of her grandfather, the well-known poet and teacher, John G. Neihardt. Seeing Dr. Neihardt's study of the mysticism of the Sioux and his scholarly experiments in the paranormal, she says, may have sensitized her to things many people don't notice, but what happened when the Frazees first bought their property was no illusion. Several events were witnessed by several people.

One notable thing happened when they added some bedrooms onto the existing house at Wildwood. To their regret, this addition closed off windows that gave a lovely view of the fields, but they had to have the living space. One morning a young girl who had spent the night with their daugh-

Then shall my ghost

come to thy bed...

what I will say,

I will not tell thee now.

John Donne, "The Apparition"

ter came to breakfast excited about something that had happened in the night. "A window slammed down inside the wall right by my bed," she said. "It woke me up."

Nobody else had heard that. The child did not know where windows had formerly been. Soon, then, the family discovered that a certain door would not stay shut, but later, when workers were razing the house, this door would not stay open. There were many such small disturbances and Lynn believes she figured out why. One day she saw an apparition, a man working in the yard around the plants, a small well-groomed man, dressed in contemporary looking clothing, but not what suggested a farmer. Something about the earnest care with which he worked suggested that maybe he was the haunting entity, someone who lingered about, from feelings of love and responsibility about the place, someone who regretted that it was being changed. Accordingly when the Frazees took the house down, they gave thought to doing it in a way that would not offend a former owner who loved it. Useful parts were salvaged, the residue burned and then buried. Nothing unusual has happened at Wildwood since.

    ℠ Ghost stories abound in Boone County, and a psychical investigator might tell us that's logical, since the area knew such intense emotional conflict during the Civil War. During this period, people who had worked hard together for the good of an area they all loved and took pride in— people who had great good will for each other—found themselves sudden enemies, or in relationships fatally strained.

During the Civil War, almost 300 men died in the Centralia Massacre, and several died at a smaller encounter at the Mt. Zion Church north of Columbia. Frequent guerrilla presence in the area also created panic. Also, a great many slaves lived in Little Dixie, frightened and resentful, yearning always for an outcome that would bring them freedom. Of course these were common feelings over the whole country during the war, but perhaps Boone County was one of those places where they were most concentrated and intense. We're told that the best ghost stories develop where history has been most dramatic.

Chapter Six

Ghosts in a Row

St. Joseph, Marceline, Paris and Hannibal are four towns in an almost straight line across the state and each of them has one or more good ghost stories. St. Joseph's ghost story is popular among investigators and Marceline's ghost has the almost unheard of distinction of supposedly killing people, while Hannibal may be nationally exclusive in staging a tour of its ghosts and haunted places.

The Scratched Cheek

This particular happening must have been exceptionally well documented at the time, perhaps by many people vouching for the honesty and stability of the family involved. Most serious reviews of credible paranormal events include this Missouri story.

A St. Louis man, identified only by the initials F.G., sat in a St. Joseph hotel room one sunny afternoon in 1876, smoking a cigar and happily writing up orders from a successful sales trip. Gradually, he became aware that he was not alone and, looking up, found his younger sister seated beside him, one of her arms resting on the table.

Hence, horrible shadow! Unreal mockery, hence!

Shakespeare, "Macbeth"

The girl had died in a cholera epidemic nine years earlier, yet she looked natural and pretty, exactly as when he last saw her in life. Mr. F.G. said he felt nothing but joy at seeing his sister and greeted her lovingly. She smiled sweetly and disappeared before his eyes. The whole incident was so brief that it was over before ink had dried on his paper. Still, F.G. took in several details. The girl's blouse was familiar to him, as were her breastpin and hair combs. To his puzzlement, there was a slight scratch on her right cheek, near her nose.

The more he thought about all this, the more alarmed the man grew. How did her cheek get scratched? It had not been that way at her funeral. What did the visit mean? There had to be some purpose for her appearance. F.G. cut his business trip short and went home to tell his parents.

Upon hearing this account, F.G.'s mother gasped. She said she had accidentally touched her daughter's face with a pin while preparing her body for burial. She concealed the scratch with powder and mentioned it to nobody, not even her husband.

The mother died suddenly two weeks later and Frederic W. H. Myers, a noted psychical researcher, wrote this in his book, *The Human Personality and Its Survival of Bodily Death:* "A clear case of a spirit's feeling her mother's approaching death...the son is brought home in time to see his mother once more, by perhaps the only means which would have succeeded. The mother is sustained, knowing that her daughter loves and awaits her."

      St. Joseph has another ghost story that has made the books. The building that served as headquarters for the Pony Express is said to be haunted, presumably by the one young man who lost his life in the 19-month existence of the daring undertaking. Riders were at such great risk from weather, injury, robbery attacks and hostile natives that the operators of the system callously wrote "orphans preferred" in their recruitment ads.

Jerry Ellis in his 1994 book, *Bareback,* described his own private re-tracing of the Pony Express trail. He said he made special arrangements to spend a night in the old depot, but aside from a hissing space heater that he at first thought might be a ghost, he heard and saw nothing unusual.

The Lethal White Lady

In 1887 when Marceline was little more than a "stomped down corn field," according to Clifford Funkhouser, a *Marceline Press* writer, the Santa Fe Railroad built a division point for routing trains to Chicago. The line brought many strangers together in a place unprepared in ways such as law enforcement, and the town gained a reputation for being a spot where, Funkhouser said, nobody thought much about it if someone died violently.

See my lips tremble

and my eyeballs roll,

Suck my last breath,

And catch my flying soul!

Alexander Pope

The story is that a certain railroad man killed a woman he'd been living with and also killed her baby, disposing of their bodies down a dry well. Old-timers were sure that the bodies rested on the site where, in 1895, a cafe called "The Hole in the Wall" operated.

A woman named Marian Roberts was the cook there for 20 years and she related strange events to the *Marceline Press* writer. First, she said, she met problems in getting employees to go into the cellar for supplies. Many left abruptly saying they heard a baby crying below, and a female voice pleading. Then came reports that a woman in a white dress sat there, glaring.

For awhile, nothing more than this happened, but in 1900, an engineer named Wise was preparing for unexpected duty, filling in for someone who could not work. The cafe's owner, Eva MacDonald, cooked him an early breakfast before the cafe opened for business, and they were talking in the kitchen as he ate. Suddenly, between them, the trapdoor to the cellar flew open and the woman in white stood there, pointing angrily at Wise. A waitress who had entered the room fainted, and Wise was so upset that he wired the railroad's roundhouse and asked to be relieved. He had to go, they told him; nobody else was available to take the train to Kansas City.

Less than an hour afterward, the train wrecked near Rothville and Wise was killed. About a year later, his brother had a similar experience, his death occurring in a wreck at Bosworth, twenty miles from Marceline. The next victim was a brakeman who saw the woman in white and before an hour had passed, died in a fall from the top of a boxcar on the Rothville Hill. The train did not wreck that time nor the next, when a trainman who had seen the apparition died on the ground, crushed between two cars.

In 1910, the ghost added something to her repertoire—or she was used as an excuse for murder. An engineer who told of meeting the woman in white left for his train anyhow, but came back into the cafe asking for help, saying the ghost had shot him. He had four bullets in his body, and in the 24 more hours he lived, insisted his assailant had been the woman in white.

That incident is much simpler than another recorded in the Marceline paper. An engineer named William Beach said he'd seen the woman in white, but successfully defied fate, he thought, making his run and returning home safely to Ft. Madison, Iowa. He went upstairs to take a bath and was found dead later with a bullet in his head. It had come through screen and window glass, angled down, from a position impossible unless one were on a high ladder. Funkhouser wrote that the snow under the window was undisturbed, with no sign of tracks, human or ladder. Neither of these two murders was ever solved, at least when these newspaper stories appeared.

The last episode blamed on the woman in white was in 1917, when a brakeman named Fletcher made fun of the ghost and descended to the

By heaven,

I'll make a ghost of him

that lets me!

Shakespeare, "Hamlet"

basement, "to have a talk with that lady." He emerged pale and shaken, unwilling to discuss what he'd seen and eager to get out of the cafe. Later that night, however, possibly drinking with friends, he regained his spirits enough to promise to attend the trainmen's New Year's Eve dance, "dead or alive." Enroute to Ft. Madison, he fell under a car and lost both legs. He died in the hospital there at about 7 p.m. which is when his roommate in Marceline came rushing into the street declaring he'd seen Fletcher's ghost.

Soon after that the cafe burned and not much later, Mrs. Roberts died. Some who have tried to analyze this story suggest that she was an unknowing channel for activity of a spirit that was finally satisfied with the revenge it had taken and accepted the fire as decent burial. Resentment on this score is, of course, considered one of the strong motivations for ghostly manifestations.

And This Lady Wore Black

The Paris ghost existed for some 70 years, according to annals of the occult. She first appeared, we're told, soon after the Civil War when many women wore the black of mourning and the dress style included deep-brimmed, concealing bonnets. Also, strangers were commonplace everywhere as people displaced by the war sought family members, and wives and parents traveled to battlefields, searching for the remains of loved ones.

The first person to see the lady in black was a young mother, calling her children in for supper. She thought only that this was someone she didn't know, a woman noticeable because she was at least six feet tall. The next night, at about the same time, the same mother and her husband, together, saw the stranger, who shook her cane at them, apparently feeling they were staring rudely. The husband said something was wrong with her and they decided to start getting the children in earlier.

Soon many Paris residents were talking of the lady in black and pooling stories. She often brandished her cane at people, and some said she walked a little above the ground, which is why she seemed so tall. Some said that from a distance her face glowed behind the veil, others that she had brushed against them as she sped past in the dark, skirts rustling. Some claimed she had peered in their windows, so everyone began to close curtains and lock doors, few venturing out at night alone for the whole winter.

With spring the woman in black no longer walked and everyone was relieved, but when fall came around again, she reappeared, and for many years this was her pattern. She never hurt anyone, but the sight of her was unsettling even to men who considered themselves brave.

The sightings stopped for good in 1934 when a 90-year-old resident died, a woman taller than average, but far from being six feet. She'd been

There are still reports that late at night
an invisible boat shoots by the docks,
lifting them high with its wake

D.W. Waldron

abandoned by her lover at the age of 19 and had lived a bitter, solitary life thereafter. A journalist who lived in Paris for several years did most of the writing about this mystery, and he suggested that the rejected spinster was the frightening lady in black. He described her as "coarse and angular." Apparently it did not occur to him that the spectral figure might have been a man, or that in a small town, residents would have thought at once of the tall and eccentric woman they all knew. Perhaps her usual appearance and demeanor were so different from the ghost's that they could not imagine her going out to frighten people.

The Town That Loves Its Ghosts

In October of 1996, an organization called Hannibal Main Street held its first Ghostly Gala, a trolley car tour of the town's oldest buildings and the sites of historic ones no longer standing. With this went a review by Kirstin Hildahl-Dewey of Hannibal's traditional ghost stories and a few new ones invented just for the occasion. From their seats, participants could look out and see embellishments of these tales—a pale, period-dressed person hurrying across the street, a silhouetted figure in a lighted window, or more than one figure, engaged in what appeared to be a life and death struggle. This just-for-fun approach does not obscure the fact that Hannibal residents describe some unexplained and unexplainable manifestations.

Jerry Adkins operates a hardware store that apparently has a benign resident ghost. Whenever something goes wrong, employees say, "It's Percy again!" They're referring to Percy Haydon, the man who in 1919 established a hardware store in a building now incorporated into Jerry's store. Percy made a great success of his store by working hard, including night hours. He was much appreciated in the community for his good selection of merchandise and fairness with customers. Jerry says, "He was a little gruff on the surface, but actually very kindhearted." Jerry remembers Percy as a heavyset man "always chewing on a stogie."

The way Percy demonstrates himself now, probably not deliberately, is by footsteps overhead in a loft where merchandise continues to be stored, or, sometimes, down on the ground floor. There are also occasional problems with the lights. They may turn themselves on again after being shut off—sometimes repeatedly in a short period of time.

The most striking event came one evening at closing time when Jerry and employee Jeanie Waters had locked the doors and were doing final work with the cash registers. They were startled by a hearty sneeze very near them and at face level. Their first thought, Jerry says, was that despite their careful check, someone still had not left the store, though that of course would not explain why the sneeze seemed to be right beside them. They

That affable, familiar ghost,

which nightly...

gulls him with intelligence...

Shakespeare, "Sonnets"

found nobody. The store has no cat, but Jerry says what they heard was much more than a cat sneeze.

Another time, another employee named Jeanie was checking doors in remote reaches of the store. It actually is made up of three buildings, some from before the turn of the century. The newest one was Percy's. She returned upset, Jerry says, because someone, from very close to her whispered urgently: "Jeanie! Jeanie!"

Though Percy has never hurt anyone, it took Jerry awhile to get used to him. In his earliest encounter with the footfalls, Jerry assumed intruders were upstairs, and called an employee to come with him to take a look.

"You're going to think I'm crazy," he apologized when he called. But stairs to the loft are right by the office door where Jerry worked. "Nobody could have come up or down without my seeing them," he said. "I've never been one to believe in ghosts," he added. "I'm not a superstitious person at all. That night, I honestly thought someone was in the store. Afterwards I didn't know what to think."

When the footsteps come down on the first floor, Jerry says he usually goes home. One night, however, from inside the restroom, he heard quite a lot of walking around and decided an employee with a key was playing a joke on him. He decided to reverse the surprise and when the footsteps paused near the restroom door, Jerry—picturing someone looking around for him—threw the door open, expecting to make that person take a gigantic jump. Nobody was there. No steps had gone away from the door. That was one of the nights when Jerry postponed his work for daytime hours.

Restorer's Hazards

Experiences of Jean and Scott Meyer, their employees and their partner, Jeff Trevathen, are not as mild as those recorded by Jerry. The Meyer's business is River City Restorations and they sometimes live in old houses while they're working on them. They have experienced several small mysteries, but the most memorable, Jean says, came one night when she was reading in bed upstairs, alone because her husband was at work in another house.

Suddenly she was shocked by two very loud, almost simultaneous crashes from the room right below her. She immediately thought of two massive pocket doors that had been taken from their niches for refinishing. They had been left leaning up against a wall and Jean was horrified, imagining an intruder downstairs had blundered into them. She phoned Scott to come home because she was afraid to go downstairs alone. Together they went through the whole house and found nothing amiss. The doors were just as they'd been left and no new tracks showed in the plaster dust that coated most of the floors.

But man dieth and wasteth away;

yea, man giveth up the ghost,

and where is he?

The Bible, Job

More than once, the Meyers have had employees who declined to work alone in the old houses, some saying they felt or heard something strange. The most remarkable story came from David Anderson, who says he went alone to the Ebert-Dulaney house one night after working hours to use some of the equipment for a home project of his own. Hearing a car stop outside and its door slam, he thought a friend had noticed his truck outside and stopped to visit. When the back door opened, he called out and then started to the hall to greet whoever it was and reassure him about the plywood that had been put across hall joists when flooring was taken up.

Before he could get there, Anderson heard the rumbling steps of someone walking across the plywood, but this stopped just short of his own door. He found the hall empty, and there had been no retreating steps. Looking out the back, he saw a neighbor on his porch which explained the car sounds, but there was no way the neighbor could have entered the house and walked the length of the hall and then gotten out and home so fast. Also, there was no inside doorway an intruder could have stepped into for concealment. Anderson said, "I put things away and went home."

The House on Maple Street

This is how Hannibal residents refer to an impressive antebellum house with an interesting history—the house is not considered haunted, exactly, just *strange*. Candace Klemenn, who has visited there often, has felt something like a current of energy that affects some of the back rooms and the back yard. Some people walk out of the affected area, saying they are nauseated or apprehensive.

"I think it's something natural," Candace said, "like earth energy or something rising from an underground stream, maybe something that somehow catches and holds emotions from the past."

She has an interest in the paranormal and has been present when sensitives tried to analyze the place. Though local history offers no details of tragedy, these people felt that something had happened at the house or near it that caused fear and suffering, something witnessed by black people, though not necessarily directed at them. Klemenn says they described a group of men, soldiers, perhaps, who were out of control, drinking, doing destructive things, and being abusive to women.

The house was occupied during the Civil War by a Commander Greene, who was in charge of some Union troops in the area. The strong Confederate sympathy around Hannibal probably made his family less than comfortable. And, it was rumored that he had something to do with the underground railway which was supported by strong abolitionist sentiment in Quincy, Illinois, just across the river. Also, Mrs. Greene supposedly taught

Some say that ever 'gainst that season comes

Wherein our Savior's birth is celebrated...

No spirit can walk abroad...

...so hallow'd and so gracious is the time.

Shakespeare, "Hamlet"

runaway slaves to read and write, and might have also given refuge to some escaping slaves via the underground railroad. Did unpleasantness arise because of all of this, maybe something life threatening?

Connection to another part of the house's history might be suspected by reaction of Klemenn's son-in-law when he was doing drywall work there. He decided not to work alone anymore because he had, first, a sensation of being watched with great interest, then the feeling that something urgently wanted him to come upstairs. This pull was so strong that he was inclined to go, in spite of his fear, but he decided to flee from the house instead.

Though the young man knew nothing of it at the time, this upstairs phenomenon could be related to a local story Klemenn had heard, of an elderly man who spent his last months bedridden in an upstairs room. He perhaps considered himself a prisoner, and he may have been, in some way. Probably no experience with the supernatural is more upsetting than the thought that someone from another dimension is pleading for help or trying to command us to perform some task long ago left undone. Klemenn speculates, "Maybe now that the house is happily occupied by a family, the ghosts can rest and let go of their hold on the premises."

Not Really Haunted

The beautiful 30-room mansion called Rockcliffe is a mecca for all who visit Hannibal. Its owners say it does not actually have any ghost stories, though they concede that before restoration it certainly looked the part. It was even considered to be haunted by neighbors. A showplace in its prime, called one of the finest houses in the United States, it had stood empty for 43 years on its hill overlooking the Mississippi River. From its balconies, one of its owners, John Cruikshank, could watch his lumber being shipped out by rail to go all over the nation. When I visited it a decade or more ago, I asked a tour guide if it had ghosts and she laughed and said, "Maybe a protective spirit of some kind, for in its empty and unprotected time, it didn't get nearly as much vandalism and damage as it could have."

Rockcliffe's remarkable features included Tiffany chandeliers and windows installed by the great artisan himself, many marble-hearthed fireplaces with hand-carved mantels, self-storing shutters that dropped down into the walls, a refrigerator room big enough to handle food for huge gatherings, and a schoolroom with a series of roll-down maps.

Though one of the present owners, Mary McAvoy, lives in the house with her husband and says they have never seen, heard or felt anything unusual, psychics who have visited Rockcliffe say they sense a discontented female presence there. This would be a safe guess, considering that many women worked at Rockcliffe as servants.

Ghosts? I don't know if I believe

in ghosts, but. . . let me tell you this . . .

a week after Bill died, some friends came to visit.

As I was talking with them . . .

all of a sudden a stack of dishes rattled loudly.

There was no physical reason for the rattling.

June Singer, " Boundaries of the Soul "

Mark Twain and Ghosts

In Rockcliffe, we might even hope to feel a little of Samuel Clemens' presence, for in 1902 at the height of his fame as Mark Twain, he's said to have stood on the beautiful staircase before the large Tiffany window. From there he addressed 300 people who had come out to honor him while he was visiting his hometown.

Clemens said he didn't believe in ghosts. He was even quoted as saying, "As you know, I'm not one of those spirit people." Yet his writings indicate a mind not totally closed on the subject, at least during part of his life. Anyone who has read much by or about Clemens remembers from *Life on the Mississippi* his account of the vivid dream which not only foretold his brother Henry's death, but accurately revealed many details about it.

Though Clemens spent most of his life outside Missouri, he was born in the small town of Florida and grew up, to the age of 22, in Hannibal. Since he traveled a great deal, he may have never spent as many years in any other one place. His writings immortalized Missouri. Clemens is not only the state's most famous literary son, but many critics feel that time will decree *Huckleberry Finn* as the greatest American novel. Surely it's appropriate to include his supernatural experiences here.

Two of his essays have "mental telegraphy" in their titles and tell how frequently ESP seemed to work for Clemens with no effort from him. He often received, in an unexpected way, just the data he needed for research. Often he ran into someone in a most unlikely place, when he'd been trying to figure out how to get in touch with that person. Letters so regularly crossed in the mail for Clemens that he had established the custom of just not mailing many of his, confident he'd not need to. He delighted in keeping his family apprised of how often this worked.

The following example of Clemens' experiences would be considered by psychical researchers a perfect example of the Doppelganger (German for "double goer") Effect, or person who is in two places at the same time. Another explanation for the following story would be that Clemens saw the apparition of a living person or had an instance of seeing something before it happened.

He wrote of being at a crowded reception preceding one of his readings and seeing a friend from the past—a woman who lived at such a distance he would never have dreamed of seeing her that day. She was attractively dressed, as always, and he took special note of her outfit, hoping he could make his way to her before his performance started. He was not able to, but when he finished, she came up to shake his hand and ask if he remembered her. He told her of seeing her earlier, and she said, "Oh, no, I

The Phantom slowly,

gravely, silently approached...

Scrooge bent down upon his knee;

for in the very air through which this Spirit moved

it seemed to scatter gloom and mystery.

Charles Dickens, "A Christmas Carol"

wasn't at the reception. I regretted missing it, but only got here in time to hear you." And there she stood before him in the dress and hat he'd so carefully studied earlier.

Clemens' most decisive experience came in Redding, Connecticut, at Christmas time of 1909, less than a year before his death. His daughter, Jean, next to the last remaining member of his family, died of an epileptic seizure in her young adulthood. Clemens, ill himself, and in shock at his loss, was not able to accompany her body for burial in another city with her mother and sister. He stood in the window and watched her coffin taken away on a snowy night and then went into the bathroom where she had died. One of Clemens' biographers, Albert Bigelow Paine, says the writer had a vague notion of telling his daughter goodbye where her life had ended. Clemens said that in the room, always a very well-heated and cozy place, he suddenly felt a cold current of air that chilled him badly. There was no place for a draft to enter and this one was only momentary. Clemens told Paine he considered it an acknowledgment from Jean.

In his autobiography account of Jean's death, Clemens said that he intended to stay in the house, because he was sure he would feel her spirit there. He told of visiting another place, then empty and in poor repair, where he had lived earlier in deep happiness when his family was complete. He said, "...to me it was a holy place and beautiful. It seemed to me that the spirits of the dead were all around me and would have welcomed and spoken to me if they could."

Chapter Seven

Riverside Ghosts

R iver towns have a special atmosphere. It lingers in their heritage of
being the first settlements, where residents pursued especially colorful occupations. Most of us are awed by the hypnotic presence of
that endless procession of powerful water—which flows from elsewhere and
moves on to elsewhere—amazing our senses just as it did those of our ancestors.

Boonville is a classic river town, settled in the early 1800s, serving as
Cooper county seat since 1818. Founders were largely Kentuckians and Vir-
ginians, with many German immigrants among the town's earliest settlers.
Boonville hosted flotillas of steamboats bedecked as ornately as wedding
cakes, and served as a departure point for pioneers heading West.

Streets are lined with wonderful old houses that saw it all, occupied by
generations of people who left their mark on Missouri. Such houses must
have ghosts, of course, and be remembered for them even when the buildings are gone. One of the best stories of this kind is often entitled, "Aunt
Eternity's Curse." It is about a Virginian named Howard Thornton Muir
whose home was rated among the most elegant mansions in Missouri. His
horses, carriages, liveried (uniformed) servants, home and lavish entertain-
ments were the grandest in the area.

Like all the powerful of his time, however, Muir was helpless against
health hazards. When his cherished daughter, Nancy, suddenly fell desper-
ately ill, difficult travel and slow communication gave no hope of getting

Fantasies...

of calling shapes and beck'ning shadows dire,

And airy tongues that syllable men's names.

John Milton, "Il Penseroso"

medical experts to her quickly. She had a fast-working malady familiar in those days: Monday, blooming health; Tuesday, chills and fever; Wednesday, delirium; Thursday or Friday, death.

The frantic family tried every home remedy they and their neighbors knew, including every suggestion of local doctors. Nothing helped. The distraught father turned in panic to Aunt Eternity, one of his oldest slaves. She was regarded by her companions as a possessor of magical healing powers. He did this reluctantly, because Aunt Eternity had more reason than just slavehood to harbor hostility for the family. Not long before Nancy's illness, the girl said she caught Aunt Eternity in some act of minor dishonesty, one version of the story says stealing a guest's silk scarf. The old woman, who had painfully, with a lifetime's work, achieved a position of importance and relatively easy tasks in the household, was demoted to the most menial and difficult, losing all of the prestige she'd had among other slaves. Despite continued suspicion, she never stopped insisting on her innocence.

No doubt Muir cautioned Aunt Eternity forcefully about what would happen to her if she tried to take revenge on Nancy, and the old woman seemed to sincerely try to save the girl's life. The illness, however, was a hopeless one and Nancy died. Apparently Muir and his wife accepted the inevitable at the time, but in the next few weeks he brooded more and more about their loss and one night, possibly when drinking, he began to wonder if Aunt Eternity might have cast the illness upon Nancy. He went to the old woman's cabin and beat her to death. In true ghost story tradition, she cursed him, his house and all of his relations as she died. And true to tradition, such calamities came upon them. In only a few years Muir was a ruined man, his family gone and his wonderful property in another's hands.

The story is not specific as to when the haunting began, whether in his own day, reducing the sale value of his house, or much later. But as everything fell into decay, people of the area reported numerous strange happenings there, including sounds and lights inside the house. The most choice manifestation was a languid, pale young woman who sometimes wandered the overgrown flower garden that had once been so beautiful. Sometimes she was seen leaning against the dry fountain and singing sadly.

This story has been retold many times. It appeared in the book *Haunted Heartland*, a widely read anthology of 1985, and many articles have featured it. *Columbia Daily Tribune* columnist Tom Ladwig went so far as to point out the location of Muir's home site, in southeast Boonville near the I-70 exit.

The late Ladwig would have debunked the story if he could, for he was a great lover of humor and irony, but he didn't know that the Aunt Eternity story is apparently a fabrication. Some researchers say there's evidence that the story was created just as an experiment to see how far it

How many children and how many men,

are afraid of ghosts,

who are not afraid of God!

T.B. Macaulay, "Dante, 1824"

would go. Shall we consider what this tells us about ghost stories in general? Or maybe just the most detailed and logical sounding ones?

The Spectral Carriage

Bob Dyer, a well-known Boonslick area historian, folklorist and songwriter, often performs a ballad which tells a tale originally collected by another respected historian and folklorist, Charles van Ravenswaay. In the 1930s, van Ravenswaay heard the story from Mrs. Hopkins, an elderly woman living near Wooldridge. With Dyer's permission, the words to the song appear here. If you want to hear him sing it, it is on a recording he made called *River of the Big Canoes*. Dyer also authored several books, one on Jesse James and the Civil War in Missouri.

The old town of Overton Landing mentioned in the song was located across the Missouri River from Rocheport. As the steamboat trade declined, so did the fortunes of the town. Eventually the remaining residents moved the town back to higher ground at the base of the river hills, where it exists to this day. Dyer believes "the house on the bluff" may have been the family home of the woman who originally told the story. He says it still stands near Wooldridge, long abandoned, with "a distinctly haunted quality about it."

    Another interesting Boonville story was told on KOMU-TV in Columbia in October 1994. Called "An Innkeeper's Tale," it concerned a woman who was caring for her aged father. The man was convinced that he could not sleep if his feet were covered up. He said this constriction made relaxation impossible for him. For a long time the daughter slipped in every night and covered his feet, unable to bear the thought of anyone, especially an elderly person, sleeping in that condition. Because her father so often woke up and protested angrily when she went in, and always had his feet uncovered in the morning anyhow, the daughter finally stopped trying. She feared her father's anger would do him as much harm as the cold, and decided maybe he was safely conditioned by a lifetime of sleeping that way.

When the daughter began to find his feet cozily tucked in each morning, she questioned him and he said wearily, "Oh, I've given up on that. That woman you send in here every night just keeps doing it and pays no attention to anything I say."

The television account ended with that statement, and we can hardly do better for an unexplainable little situation.

Arrow Rock

Arrow Rock is another place so rich in history one doesn't know where to begin. With settlement beginning in 1815, it became a flourishing

The Phantom Black Carriage
Song by Bob Dyer

There once was a town called Overton Landing;
Back in the days of the steamboat trade.
It was down in the bottoms on the banks of the river,
And just like the steamboat it faded away.
And there's nothing left now but the story
Of the people who lived in a house on the bluff above town,
And a phantom black carriage, and a woman in a black silk gown.

The house on the bluff had once been a mansion,
But the fortune that built it had dwindled away,
And now it was old like the people who lived there,
A tumble-down dream of the glittering days.
And the old man dreamed of the glory,
The old woman dreamed of the good times she'd known long ago,
And a shiny black carriage, and a black silken gown she once wore.

A stranger came looking for shelter one evening.
His carpet-bag was filled with silver and gold.
They killed him for his money and they threw him in the river
'Cause they knew that his story would never be told.
And then they said that they'd gotten their fortune
From a relative who died in a city way down in the South,
And they got the black carriage, and the old woman got her black gown.

But then one day the woman took a fever;
There wasn't any doctor who could figure out why.
She made the old man swear he'd never remarry
If it turned out this was her time to die.
And then she died that very next morning.
The old man put her in her casket in her black silk gown,
And he put the black carriage out back behind the old smoke house.

Well, now the old man he had all of the money,
And everything he touched seemed to turn to gold.
He went to the city and he met a younger woman.
She followed him back to his country home.
But on the night of the day they got married,
As the old man was seeing the last of the guests back to town,
There came a phantom black carriage, and a woman in a black silk gown.

The man's young wife she looked out of the window.
She saw him standing on the front porch stair,
And then from the shadows came a phantom black carriage.
The man got in, and the carriage disappeared.
It's been a long time now since it happened.
There's nothing left now of the house on the bluff or the town,
But people still see the carriage, and a woman in a black silk gown.

commercial port with a stable population of 1,000, augmented each year by thousands of travelers and river workers. Famous residents have included the painter George Caleb Bingham and Dr. John Sappington, whose research was vital in conquering malaria. Arrow Rock also raised Missouri three state governors.

The town has now shrunk to include only about 70 residents, but its charm still attracts thousands of visitors each year. The Lyceum Theater, its repertory theater, is active every summer and the town teems with craft shows, festivals and historical tours. With antique shops, excellent restaurants and several bed and breakfasts, Arrow Rock is always in the process of doing more restoration. Naturally, this is a place ghosts cannot resist.

A favorite spot apparently is The Old Tavern, built in the early 1830s by slaves working for a Virginian named John Huston. The tavern still operates as a fine restaurant. The Old Tavern's present manager, Bunny Thomas, has lived there for four years and says, "I love it, and have never been afraid, but some people won't go upstairs." Her daughter, she says, would never stay in the building alone at night and a teenager who mopped the floors for them quit, saying that when every other room was empty and he was in the kitchen, he could hear eating and talking in the dining room. He even heard his own named called out.

Bunny has heard her name called out too, from the front when she's in the kitchen and vice versa. Once, she says, she was greeted as she came through the swinging door into an empty dining room, by a male voice saying in flirtatious tones, "Well, hello there!"

Her most memorable experiences, though, came in 1981, when she worked as floor manager and was given an upstairs apartment to live in. The very first night she saw smoke in her bedroom and went downstairs in panic, only to find no sign or smell of fire anywhere. Creakings and other sounds were so constant that Bunny kept the radio on to drown them out.

One odd and interesting event starred an old dog whose owner had died. Though nobody officially adopted this animal, he was not a stray. He was the town dog—he ate at several places and was petted by everyone. His habit was to visit the tavern's back door every night for whatever he might find there, and he would hang out for awhile with Bunny, then go on his way or perhaps sleep near the building. Bunny never brought him inside and he never seemed to have any desire to come in.

One night they had finished their usual routine and Bunny had gone up to bed. At some point she was wakened by a scratching on her door, but supposing it was just one of the ghosts, she turned the radio up louder and went back to sleep. The next morning, when she opened her apartment door, the town dog uncurled himself from the hall carpet and greeted her.

They are the results of suppressed desires. . .
the ripples on the surface of life,
produced by unsuspected springs.
And these may be very deep—
as deep as the soul itself.

Joseph Campbell, "The Hero with a Thousand Faces"

"I always try to figure out how things could have happened," she said, "but I never could see any way he could have got in. If he had his own entrance, why did he use it only that once?" And she adds that her employers, Clay Marsh and Chet Breitwieser, who are something of pranksters, promised her solemnly that they would never do anything to frighten her. "I believe them," she said. "I've never had any reason not to."

Another odd occurrence involved an element of The Old Tavern's decor, a display of historic documents. One time a visitor whose ancestors had lived in Arrow Rock found something pertaining to his family and wanted to photograph it. Light inside being inadequate for his Polaroid camera, Bunny went into the lobby with him to hold the paper where proper exposure would be possible. When the picture was developed, it showed not the printed material, but a picture of a log cabin. There was no such structure within the camera's range.

℘   Ghosts also seem to dwell also in some of Arrow Rock's private homes. One of these, among the town's oldest, has a small upstairs room the present tenant uses for sewing and as a guest room. Some of her guests decline to sleep in it. One is her daughter—a tax accountant—who refuses to even enter the room alone. Another is a black Labrador dog belonging to the householder's son. Though the man has slept there without incident, the dog, who shares his room everywhere else, resolutely stays in the hall.

The owner never saw or felt anything in the room, but her daughter once reported a crowding presence against her in the doorway, as if someone was rudely pushing past.

St. Charles

St. Charles is a highly historic town, too. It was our first state capital and the place where leaders met to do work necessary for gaining statehood and then to draft a state constitution. Many famous men traveled to St. Charles to participate in these important efforts. Many people who became vital to Missouri's history first stepped onto its soil from riverboats docking there. The town is rich in lovingly restored buildings and one group of them in the southeastern part of town offers a variety of wares and services. Here are a few of the incidents reported by John R. Dengler for *St. Charles Life Magazine*—things that happened on his property and to his neighbors on South Main Street.

An employee came tearing down the stairs of The Farmer's Home, a former inn which now houses both Dengler's home and his tobacco store; she said someone touched her gently on the shoulder. For about four days, a French-speaking entity played tricks with cigarettes, hiding them or float-

Perfume Ghosts appear
in the form of a phantom fragrance
that is immediately identifiable
with someone who has died.

Anonymous

ing packs in the air; on the fifth day of his visit, a baby was heard crying and then quieted by soothing French words. Sometimes heavy booted footsteps pace the halls and stairs of this house and sometimes the enticing aroma of green beans and ham wafts from what was the ladies' dining room a century or more ago. A daughter of the Dengler family was once startled by a hearty and very close-by male laugh when she was alone in the guest room.

The history of his house, Dengler says, includes ownership first by a Frenchman, then later by Alexander McNair, the state's first governor, a man who had 27 tanning vats on the property. Another tenant was a woman named Lizette Waye, whose eight-year-old daughter died suddenly there. Almost every human drama imaginable must have been played out among all those who stayed here when Farmer's Home was an inn.

     80   One of Dengler's neighbors often sees poltergeist-like movements of merchandise in her shop. Sometimes these are seen by customers, and once an explosive sound from the ceiling put everyone on the floor in terror. A cause could never be found.

     80   Aimless movements in a place called The Button Shop suggest to the owner a bored child flicking display racks into motion and doing anything else it could think of for a little action. This proprietor found that she can stop the annoyance by saying sharply, "Quit that!"

     80   Donna Hafer, owner of a restaurant called the Mother-In-Law House told Dengler a strange story of how mishaps seemed to constantly occur on the north side of her building. Phenomena included spilled water and coffee, sometimes on guests, food that was unaccountably hot when it should be cold or vice versa and sudden disappearances of supplies.

A psychic advised redecorating the space with happier colors to overcome a negative imprint made by the spirit of the builder's mother-in-law, who had spent much time sitting in her rocker in that area, feeling forlorn and unwanted. She was hurt, no doubt, that her son-in-law's condition for her living near her daughter was that she have entirely separate quarters. Hafer was also told to try to extend love to this lonely spirit. These suggestions seemed to solve the problems.

Dengler speculated that all these happenings might stem from the 1789 St. Charles Borromeo Cemetery which once occupied nearby land. Moving its bodies—those that could be found, considering that many had been transients buried without stones—to another cemetery a mile or so away may have left some disturbed spirits.

Chapter Eight

Otherworldly Others

M any of Missouri's good ghost stories stand alone, not particularly associated with an area or a category. Two of these are from Maries County, near Vienna, one very old and one more recent, told by people who experienced them firsthand.

The oldest story stars an elderly man who had never subscribed to any religious belief. This made him the favorite target of a certain circuit rider (preacher who went from church to church on a regular schedule) who felt obliged to save the soul of every nonbeliever. The old farmer always tried to be polite, but finally lost patience with the persistent minister and said, "I'll tell you what. If you can prove to me that there's any form of life after death, I'll be baptized." This not only quieted the preacher for the moment; he never came back. The farmer congratulated himself on being rid of a nuisance until the community eventually learned that the preacher had died.

One evening as the elderly couple sat on their porch, the preacher came riding up the lane, wearing his usual wide-brimmed hat. His satchel, as always, flapped from the saddle horn. "They were wrong about him dying," the wife said. The evangelist dismounted and stood at the gate, as if ready to raise a loop of wire holding it shut. Then, instead, he just looked at

Aurora's harbinger, at whose approach,
ghosts wandering here and there
troop home to churchyards.

Shakespeare, "A Midsummer Night's Dream"

them with a big, triumphant smile and turned back to his horse as if to climb on. Man and animal gradually faded to invisibility. The storyteller did not know whether the aged agnostic went to church as a result of this visit.

The other Vienna story concerned a log house that had belonged to a couple named Gib and Nettie Helton. Gib was a fiddle player and passersby were accustomed to hearing his music. A number of them claimed they still heard it, throughout the many years his widow lived there alone.

This did not disturb a young man named John Malone, who bought the old house, four rooms, two-over-two, with a lean-to kitchen. He reworked the place extensively, enlarging it and, among other things, replacing the steep, narrow corner staircase with a wider one more conveniently located. While working on the house he lived in it, and he told his family of hearing a number of inexplicable sounds from upstairs. Nothing seemed menacing, but despite repeated investigations, he still found no causes. What he heard most often was the latch working on the now nonexistent staircase door, and the sound of footsteps going up or coming down.

Malone's widow, Kathryn, who now lives in Jefferson City, says she never heard that particular sound. She heard nothing that seemed danger-ous to her or their three daughters. The girls, sleeping dorm style in a big upstairs room, reported a few puzzling little things. Once it was what they said "looked like a pillow slip floating around." The only adult who felt alarmed there was Lois Malone, John's mother. She said she dreaded baby sitting in the house because it had sounds "like someone throwing boxes down the stairs."

The couple left this house and moved to Jefferson City when their girls were school age. The house eventually burned down.

A Sinister Hill

Knob Noster's curiosity is best related in *Haunted Heartland* which de-votes a long story to the fearsome stranger who came to the area well before the Civil War and lived like a hermit up on "the knob," the hill from which the town gets its name. When the hermit visited the town for sup-plies, he spoke no unnecessary words and seldom looked anyone in the face. Something about him frightened almost everyone. Children needed no urging to keep their distance.

Surprisingly, this man had a slave who was very pleasant and friendly and—to the town's relief—usually did the hermit's trading and errands. People commented that they felt sorry for anyone who was slave to such a person as the hermit and when the black man stopped coming, wondered if his owner had done him in. When the old man resumed his own shopping, someone was bold enough to ask what happened to his nice servant. He didn't an-

Do you hear those little chirps and twitters

coming out of that piece of apple-wood?

Those are the ghosts of the robins and blue-birds

that sang upon the bough

when it was in blossom last spring.

Thomas Bailey Aldrich, "Miss Mehitabel's Son"

swer and after that appeared less and less often. At last people were sure he had died or moved away.

Then came a summer of drought so terrible nobody could think of much else. The damage to crops and livestock hurt the community beyond anything anyone had ever seen. When relief finally came, it was through an equally remarkable storm. Nobody could remember such torrents of rain, such terrifying thunder and lightning. Only a few even had the nerve to look out their windows at it, but some who did reported seeing, between the blasts of lightning, a dim, swinging light, like a lantern, slowly descending the knob. "It's the old hermit," they told each other. "Maybe his house got struck or maybe he just got so scared he didn't want to be alone."

After one especially close and long-lasting barrage, they looked out again and saw no little light. Had the old man been hit by lightning?

The next day a few men ventured up the hill, and according to accounts written by authors Beth Scott and Michael Norman, the men said they found their unloved neighbor dead, with no sign of being injured in any way. Yet his face, they said, was "so contorted with fear that the men staggered back in horror." After that, on stormy nights, residents of Knob Noster declared they could see a faint, swinging light during pauses between lightning flashes.

Elusive Ladies

The affinity of college girls for ghosts seems unquenchable. Most schools have eerie stories—especially those in historic towns. Lindenwood College in St. Charles, founded in 1853 as the first college for women west of the Mississippi, has a few ghost stories that involve elusive ladies.

There's something about someone who hanged herself in a tower room. It's also said that the cofounder, Mary Sibley, still plays the organ, and is responsible for instances of good luck—because she assured the girls before she died that she would always watch over Lindenwood. Closer to her departure from this world, she said, "My spirit will always be with you." She remains on campus to this day, buried near her family in a small cemetery there.

The Sibley home constituted the school's first residence hall and its replacement is still in use. It was the scene of the school's best-developed ghost story. One recent summer when the campus was almost empty, Sibley Hall was being exhaustively renovated. There was no reason for anyone but workmen to be near it, and they came and went by the front entrance, taking care that no other doors be unlocked. One day, between the noises of their own equipment, they heard feminine voices from above from time to time, and loud clunking sounds like drawers being opened and closed, and screeching sounds like trunks being dragged around.

A vague mist hanging 'round half the pages:
(Sometimes how strange and clear to the soul,
That all these solid things are indeed
but apparitions, concepts, nonrealities).

Walt Whitman, "Leaves of Grass"

At quitting time, one or two of the men went up to make sure the ladies could get out and knew to be sure and lock up well. They found nobody there, no furniture and no trunks. A search of all floors, all vacant, gave no hint of how those sounds could have been made.

If someone wanted to invent a likely ghost story for Lindenwood, it could feature the sound of galloping hooves at night and the sobs of a bereaved woman, for the Sibleys were close friends of Elijah Lovejoy, the determined abolitionist who crusaded with his newspaper until he was killed in Alton, Illinois, in November 1837. History says that once when Lovejoy was on a lecture tour in Missouri, his enemies plotted to kill him. Sibley offered refuge at the college and, when escape back to Alton was feasible, provided Lovejoy with a horse. After the activist's death, the Sibleys were among those who helped Lovejoy's expectant widow return to her parents in St. Charles. Almost certainly she was in their home at some time with her grief and outrage. Perhaps these events have their part in whatever haunts Lindenwood.

In "The Woods"

Shannon Graham of Jefferson City was a student at William Woods College in Fulton, in the 1940s. She says the college had a ghost whose presence had something in common with the grey lady of Christian College: she was felt, rather than seen. Her movements came at dinnertime each evening, when the students and faculty ate together in Jones Hall. Yet, as memories of her fade, she appears less and less.

"Promptly at 6:45 p.m., total silence and a coldness would descend on the entire group," Graham recalled. "No one needed to look at her watch. Shaky smiles were exchanged, but no conversation." The seniors made sure younger girls knew that this was the spirit of a student who died there decades earlier, by some mysterious accident. In the years right after her death, she was sometimes seen as "a small figure with long dark hair in a filmy dress," Graham said.

Many students believe that as the number of people who remember a ghost diminish, it loses its power to manifest. If that's true, probably few people now at the college have even heard the story, let alone seen any such manifestations. But Graham declares something was there in her time. She adamantly stated, "It was not imagination."

The Wayward Elevator

Central Missouri State at Warrensburg also has its apparent hauntings, some similar to those in other schools. A young man who attended there only a few years ago relates the college's most intriguing haunts:

*I drew my blanket over my face
and tried to think of Christmas.
But the grey face still followed me.
It murmured; and I understood
that it desired to confess something.*

James Joyce, "Dubliners"

In the 1980s, during stressful exams week, a student named Sarah killed herself on the fourth floor of Houts-Hosey Residence Hall. So many strange things happened there afterward that nobody wanted to live even on the third floor and the building was closed for a time for remodeling. When it reopened, spaces had been altered and rooms renumbered haphazardly, going from Room 8 to Room 11 to Room 3 and so on, so no one could tell any longer which room had been Sarah's.

My narrator lived in Houts-Hosey Hall and was a resident monitor entrusted with various keys and the authority to deal with and prevent problems. Oddities he witnessed included a supply closet light that was on almost every time he unlocked the door, despite his care of always turning it off. Residents, he says, were accustomed to doors slamming down a hallway in quick succession when few people were present and no windows were open to create drafts. Those who played with Ouija boards reported they were frighteningly active, he said, without explaining further. He refused to speculate on the outcome of these sittings.

In one hair-raising episode, he was with a few others in the building during a school break when the campus was almost empty. Over their heads they heard what he terms "a ruckus," that sounded as if a number of people were hastily moving furniture. Desks screeched across linoleum floors. Chairs dragged about. Doors opened and closed. The sounds lasted only a minute or so, but when the alarmed listeners got upstairs, they found everything in several rooms had been pushed to the center. This left them baffled and uneasy. It would have taken many people to do this work in the brief time the sounds had lasted. They tried recreating this event and were unable to make the same changes so quickly. Nobody could be found in the completely locked building.

Another memorable experience was shared by several people who got on an old elevator on the ground floor to go to the second. The device had never malfunctioned before, but that night it took them immediately to the basement, where its door refused to open. After a short stay there, in response to their frantic pushing of the second floor button, it went to the haunted top floor, and paused there for some time, door locked. At last it took them back to the ground floor where they gratefully jumped out and ran up the stairs, never again to trust the elevator.

∞   Something else interesting at Warrensburg, quite apart from the college, is a tombstone at a nearby cemetery that glows weirdly from a distance, but seems to lose its luminescence as one approaches it. The eerie green glow can best be registered when not looking directly at the stone, and continues to occur both when there is a full moon and even on the

Here dwelt the spirit haunted

By a demoniac throng.

John Henry Bonner,
"Poe's Cottage at Fordham"

darkest of nights. This phenomenon has been noted in "Ripley's Believe It or Not" without further explanation. One's first thought is that the stone must be made of a composition different from other tombstones, but wouldn't we expect all the stones in a cemetery to come from the same supplier who used the same material? A similar stone has been reported in Hermann and in neither case is there any local story to explain the glow.

Another Vengeful Wife

Angry spouses are common in ghost stories, but Missouri has one with a unique twist. The book *Haunted Heartland* used a Kirksville story that began in 1873 with the death of a woman named Harriet Burchard. She had been a most possessive wife, considering her husband so attractive he could hardly be risked out of her sight. Burchard accepted this with flattered amusement and never gave her any cause to distrust him. He was kind and attentive through her illness, and stayed committed until her demise.

After her departure, however, he waited only five months before marrying again. He chose a younger and prettier wife named Catherine. One day, about three weeks after the wedding, when Catherine was home alone, she was terrified to hear what sounded like a rain of large rocks on the roof. A look outside proved it to be just that—the yard and roof were cluttered with rocks large enough to do damage where they fell. When they began to rise up for another onslaught, she ran back into the house and cowered until Burchard returned. His inspection showed no unusual number of rocks on the property, and he teased her a little about her fears.

A night or two later, though, Burchard was aroused from sleep by the bedcovers being roughly snatched off him and thrown on the floor. It could not have been Catherine kicking in her sleep since she lay beside him as peaceful as an angel. No draft could possibly have lifted so many quilts. He reorganized the bed, tucking everything in firmly at sides and bottom.

Just when he was almost asleep, Burchard's pillow was yanked from beneath his head. Quite sure now that Catherine was doing this to get even with him for disbelieving her rock story, he stood staring at her intently, for some sign she was actually awake. Thus, he got to witness her pillow being pulled away so rudely that she awoke screaming.

These attacks became routine with Burchard, who predictably, became an insomniac. He was thankful that Catherine slept through everything after that first night. Finally, one event removed any doubt as to who the spirit was. While he was reading in bed, the covers rolled slowly away from him as if by human hands, and on the sheet in front of him appeared a message. "These things will continue forever." The handwriting was that of his deceased wife, Harriet.

The houses are haunted

by white night gowns.

None are green, or purple with green rings,

or green with yellow rings. . .

None of them are strange. . .

Wallace Stevens, "Disillusionment of Ten O'Clock"

Justice on Back Order

The book *Historic Haunted America*, by the same team who did the *Haunted Heartland* books, reports of a peddler named Samuel Moritz who stopped regularly in Laclede County, in the Lebanon area, in the years just before the Civil War. One time, when his pack was almost empty and he was heading home, he went to spend the night with a farmer named Baker. Traveling in the dark was, of course, foolish for a peddler who had obviously sold all of his wares and would be considered to be carrying a tidy sum of money. Nobody thought anything about not seeing Moritz again, assuming he'd just gone on his way the next morning and found a more profitable route for subsequent trips.

A few years later, however, on a moonlight night, a local minister named Cummings was driving home in his buggy when he crossed a certain bridge and was surprised to see a man with a pack and a sturdy walking stick. The man was peering about anxiously, one version of this story being that he was pointing under the bridge.

Cummings stopped and offered the man a ride. The man did not answer, but looked at him and pointed more emphatically with his stick. Thinking the peddler might be deaf, the pastor climbed from his buggy and leaned down to talk louder, but the man moved out of sight. Then the minister's reliable old horse unaccountably began to plunge around, obviously spooked. By the time he got his horse under control, and looked back, the stranger had completely vanished. Yet when Cummings looked again, the man had resumed his position, pointing under the bridge.

This incident troubled Cummings all night and the next day he told a neighbor about it. Fearing the man had been mute and had been trying to point out someone in trouble, they went to the bridge and there found farmer Baker hanged from one of the supports. As they clambered around on the muddy bank, trying to get him down, they dislodged a great deal of soil and rock and to their horror, found human remains. Some clothing was left, or possibly the peddler's pack, and they could recognize Moritz.

The question then became whether the peddler had haunted Baker all that time, perhaps driving him to dig into the bank and make sure the body was still there, or whether conscience had just preyed on Baker until he went and killed himself at the scene of his crime. In any case, said the writers, the peddler had had his revenge.

Chapter Nine

In the City

T hough we think of ghosts as preferring isolation and silence, big cities must have special attractions for spirits. Both St. Louis and Kansas City have some of the best ghost stories one could hope for. Beginning with westward expansion, people of different ethnic groups and
backgrounds arrived, fortunes were made quickly, and elaborate houses were
constructed that sheltered generations of families—many of which saw great
success and great tragedy.

A *St. Louis Globe-Democrat* article for Halloween 1978 listed seven St.
Louis buildings with a reputation for being haunted. Another, in an undated clipping, stars six entirely different houses and discusses ghosts connected with the Missouri and Mississippi Rivers. Anthologies of ghost stories always include St. Louis. The Lemp Mansion has special fame, being
one of *Life Magazine*'s "Nine Most Haunted Houses in the U.S.," a designation given in 1980. The Lemp Mansion hauntings are dealt with at length
in another chapter of this book. Meanwhile, here are some other interesting sites and events:

A voice in hollow murmurs

through the courts,

Talks of a nameless deed.

Ann Radcliffe, "The Mysteries of Udolpho"

Daddy's Girl

A sad little 1989 *Post-Dispatch* story told of a child who wandered staircases for many decades in a luxurious home known as "The Castle," in the Central West End. Her plaintive cries of "Daddy! Daddy!" had been attested to by several people. She was thought to be the ghost of Jacob Goldman's youngest child, Hortense, who had died shortly before he built and moved to the mansion. Despite his wealth, Goldman had been able to do little to compensate Hortense for losing her mother at the age of four, and then, when she herself sickened only two years later, no power on earth could save her.

The father's story had other sad aspects. He was a German who came to this country as an almost penniless teenager before the Civil War and somehow managed to make a fortune in cotton in the southern states. When Goldman came to settle in St. Louis he owned half of the world's largest cotton company but, because he was Jewish, was nonetheless barred from building in the rich and fashionable areas of Westmoreland Place and Portland Place.

Goldman bought a large tract between Kingshighway and Euclid, naming it Hortense Place. Several well-known people built lavish homes there including Albert Lambert, heir to the Listerine fortune, later honored by having the airport named for him. Goldman's own Carthage stone palace contained the biggest ballroom in the city, and invitations to dance there were highly coveted. He spent $35,000 to furnish the house, a fortune at the time, and remained there until 1930 with his three other children from the wife he had lost in 1894. Whether or not they heard Hortense's cries was not part of the story; perhaps she was contented there until her family left the house.

The next owner of The Castle was Henry Miller, who modernized it according to standards of the era. It was his servants who first discovered the presence of a little girl searching the stairs for her father. Sold again in the 1940s, and converted to a rooming house, The Castle began to decline; in the 1960s vandals damaged it badly and took away its chandeliers and mantel pieces. In the 1970s, however, the house was renovated and became a private home once more. Whether or not Hortense continued her search through all this, she was active again in the 1980s, when guests heard her questing voice and remarked to their host that they'd not known he had a child. He had none.

This touching story is unusual in that Hortense seemingly followed her father to a home where she had never lived and clung to him there.

If pursued at night by an evil spirit,
or the ghost of one dead,
and you hear foot steps behind you,
try and reach a stream of running water,
for if you can cross it, no devil or ghost
will be able to follow you.

Lady Wilde, "Irish Mystic Charms & Superstitions"

An Awful Story from Webster Groves

The book *Historic Haunted America* tells of the Furry family who bought a pleasant two-story frame and brick house on Plant Avenue in Webster Groves and experienced terrors later studied deeply by psychical investigators.

The earliest event was Mrs. Furry waking at about 2 a.m. with the unpleasant feeling of having been shaken. This happened repeatedly. Once she was wakened by what sounded and felt like a strong hammer blow on the headboard. Then, each day about sunrise, she began hearing footsteps of children running up and down the stairs, rapidly and confidently, as if on familiar ground. She mentioned none of this to her husband for some time, certain that since they slept apart, he'd have heard nothing and would not believe her. But as oddities continued and grew more unpleasant, Mrs. Furry decided she had to leave. When she told her husband, he admitted having heard some strange things himself, but supposed they were natural to the house. Soon thereafter, he saw a translucent shape in his bedroom and as it drifted out, he followed it to a child's room.

Though the children made their own reports, such as "a woman who hits me with a broom, but it doesn't hurt," the Furrys stayed in the house for several years. They sold it without relating their experiences to anyone.

The next occupation was by a family named Whitcomb, who only rented the house. Mrs. Whitcomb, who was interested in the supernatural, later said she sensed a strangeness there from her first entrance and was not surprised to see misty human-like shapes and to feel unexplainable drafts.

The only manifestation to really disturb her was a baby's crying. When her children began asking questions about running footsteps on the stairs, Mrs. Whitcomb undertook to research the house, starting with neighbors. They told her it had belonged to a man named Henry Gehm, who was involved with circuses. For reasons not fully explained, they'd concluded that Gehm kept assorted valuables in his home and that the disturbances were related to his guarding these or searching for them.

This didn't seem to fit very well into what was happening, but Mrs. Whitcomb began keeping a journal of happenings. These were some of the most varied ever recorded in one place. Entries included a musty odor that came and went, as well as footsteps in the attic heard by all family members at the same time. Often they felt strong urges to go to the attic and when they did, always found things out of order, different from their last visit. Sometimes storage boxes and trunks were open, with contents strewn around. Most affectingly, a doll house outgrown by the Whitcombs' youngest daughter was once pulled out into a more accessible location and the dust around it was full of little bare footprints.

I wonder myself where it all began.

We start up in the mists of mystery,

and there we all end.

And souls drift like fog

across a hundred worlds and far frontiers.

Richard Peck, "Ghosts I Have Been"

Other happenings were routine for haunted houses: lights went on and off, objects flew through the air and the Whitcombs' neatly organized desk drawers were stirred into chaos. But not all activity was destructive. Once a defunct old music box they'd kept for sentiment's sake was suddenly and permanently repaired. Further questioning of neighbors convinced the Whitcombs that no pranks were involved. They could only conclude they were sharing the house with a discarnate family that resented them and wanted them out. On the day they obliged, it was to the accompaniment, even as they carried their own possessions down, of children running at furious speed up and down beside them on the stairs and by the sound of voices, something they'd never heard before.

The National Directory of Haunted Places, by Dennis William Hauck, varies from Norman and Scott by saying Henry Gehm was a German immigrant who built the house in the 1890s and lived a reclusive life in it until he died alone there in the early 1950s. Among experiences Hauck listed for later residents were sounds like birds hitting windowpanes and a ghostly lady in black who moved about surrounded by a white cloud. He refers to a Walsh family, saying they saw the black lady and also a small blonde girl. In March of 1966, Hauck says, Gehm's ghost appeared to Mrs. Walsh and directed her to a secret chamber, possibly once the location of his treasure, but completely empty when she looked in.

A Diaphanous Gown

A more recent and modish apparition was reported several times in Room 304 of the Chase Hotel in St. Louis, starting in 1980. A typical experience, shared by a salesman for a *Post-Dispatch* Halloween feature: he entered his room one night to find a lovely young lady with glamorously arranged red hair standing at the window, looking musingly down at traffic below. When she turned and smiled hazily at him, he assumed she had somehow arrived at the wrong place and tried, pleasantly and politely, to dismiss her. She neither replied nor moved as he explained that he needed rest and privacy. Eventually, embarrassed and angry, he phoned the desk, only to hear, "...no problem. She'll probably be gone when you turn around." And indeed she was.

Not all who saw this charming ghost were men traveling alone. Women were visited too, and at least once a couple described as "a well-known entertainer and his wife" saw her. Sometimes the apparition just stood near the bed, smiling. Sometimes she made her exit through a closed door.

Nobody at the Chase could offer any explanation. Nobody knew of any young woman who had lost her life there. They only knew that all who saw the phantom commented on her beauty and a gown variously described

There's one hour every day

when ghost-seers can see spirits

—but only one. At no other time

have they the power,

yet they never know the hour,

the coming of it is a mystery.

Lady Wilde, "Irish Mystic Charms & Superstitions"

as white chiffon or as "...filmy...full and fluffy...like a showgirl...glittery...sort of transparent but not revealing..."

Some St. Louis Short Shorts

Newspapers in 1908 and for years after, reported a West End ghost, near Easton and Kingshighway, which began just as "a big noise" and later became a veiled and black-gowned lady who languished along a staircase and played poignant tunes on the piano. Supposedly the landlord denied her existence bitterly, saying someone just wanted to devalue his property. A tenant said she'd heard enough odd sounds, such as footsteps where nobody was walking, to make her spend most nights with friends and relatives. When interviewed, she'd slept in her own apartment only four nights of the past fourteen. What she'd heard from the piano, she said, was at times almost a tune, but usually sounded more like a cat or parrot walking over the keys.

    🔊   Another West End home, on Maryland Avenue, was visited in January of 1967 by Joan Foster Dames of the *Post-Dispatch* staff. The owner had reported footsteps to the third floor from an invisible climber and a mournful upstairs presence that made people's hair bristle. The family's Chihuahua, Ginger, was often upset for no reason anyone could see, but the spirits were at least apparently harmless. Thorough research of the house revealed no past tragedy. No previous owner claimed to have experienced anything strange. Guests complained of being pushed out of bed, so the couple spent a night on the third floor. The woman slept well, but the husband said he was awakened several times by someone punching him. Dames took a light view of all this, mentioning how many times they referred to their Chihuahua's reactions to the spirit they called "Old Chap." She concluded, "A Chihuahua is not what one usually calls a reliable witness."

    🔊   A childish apparition whose audacity included appearing at a child's party finally exasperated the long-suffering mother of a certain St. Louis family. She had felt sympathy for the little ghost even though its appearances usually were followed by troublesome blood stains on the carpet. But one day when her own children were elsewhere, and upstairs romping got too loud, according to *Post-Dispatch* writer, Jim Creighton, the mother ended it permanently, without knowing she could do so. She shouted angrily, "You're dead! You're dead! Go away!" Creighton's experts told him this was a case of the child not knowing she was dead until informed of that fact. Something to remember, perhaps, for ghostly encounters!

May no ill dreams disturb my rest,

Nor powers of Darkness me molest.

Evening Hymn

Near St. Louis

St. Louis resident Hella Canepa told an interesting story she discovered in researching a resort hamlet, Castlewood, near St. Louis. A wealthy man contracted to buy a luxurious house on blufftop acreage there with a wonderful view of the Meramec River. He soon decided, "...this house is haunted...full of ghosts."

As Canepa quoted him: "Things happen all day long, strange noises I can't locate, objects inexplicably moved to crazy places, my dog yelping or growling for no reason, intense creepy feelings, a sudden draft or stench from no apparent source. I keep a horse out there and it won't come near the house...

"But the really bizarre stuff starts at night...I'm awakened by the same three notes played on a violin. Can you imagine? It's loud, right in the room with me. Then it's gone and there's nothing but silence again.

"Of course I can't fall asleep again. I get up and go to the kitchen or bathroom...and the 'parties' start. All of a sudden, sounds of laughter, music, lively conversation and activity surround me. I look all over the house but can never find where it's coming from before it stops. This also happens when I come home late at night."

A psychic who visited the house told the man she felt "an unbearable sense of horror and impending doom." She was sure that somebody—maybe several people—met their end there suddenly and violently. She suggested that he move at once. He later learned that the house was built on the spot where a hotel had burned more than fifty years earlier. If Canepa researches this further, she may find that many people died in the fire, or that no one was ever sure whether all of the bodies were found.

Kansas City

Among Kansas City's best known haunted places are the castle-like Epperson House on the University of Missouri campus, areas of The Radisson Muhlebach Hotel, Loretto School auditorium, and the Spanish Chapel in the Nelson Art Galley.

Kansas City also has one particularly detailed and unique story, about a house that happily sheltered a family for decades, yet when the parents were gone, turned unkindly on their daughter. This appeared in *Star Magazine* in 1987, in a Halloween article by John Hughes.

For over all there hung a cloud of fear,

a sense of mystery the spirit daunted,

and said as plain as whisper in the ear,

"The place is haunted."

Thomas Hood

The Hostile House

Neither past nor present owners of the house wanted to be identified, so Hughes gave the name "Maggie" to the daughter. Her father had died peacefully, but Maggie's mother then killed herself, by asphyxiation with the car.

While recovering from these traumatic events, Maggie had two friends with her, one at night and the other by day. Neither was an addict, she said, and neither had any interest in the supernatural, but one said she saw Maggie's parents and was instructed by the mother to go out and buy Maggie a dogwood tree. Maggie took this as a direct message, for shortly before her mother's death, the two of them had discussed whether or not a dogwood from further south could survive in Missouri. This was the trivial sort of exchange nobody would bother to share with anyone else and Maggie hadn't.

   The other friend, on a day when Maggie was away, heard a noise in the garage and when she went to check found the car motor running, all doors locked and no ignition key. Among other things Maggie found she could not live with: books and other objects rising from their places and falling loudly to the floor, her dog sitting up in bed and moving its head to intently watch something that seemed to be moving across the room, the fragrances of food in the kitchen on the day of the week Maggie's mother had always grocery shopped, door knobs that turned when nobody was there. A friend asked about the woman she'd seen primping at a hall mirror; another friend said she heard faint cries of "Help me! Help me!"

When Maggie had a group of psychics in, they said they found nothing of significance, though one of them accurately described Maggie's grandmother whose disposition had been unpleasant. After they left, Maggie and a friend were terrified by two loud crashes, each hard enough to shake the house. They called the psychics, who interpreted this as proof of an unearthly presence and as a sign of anger at being investigated.

Buyers for this house reported no disturbances for several months, but did eventually call and ask Maggie for the psychic's phone number.

The Epperson House

The Epperson House, originally built in the early 1920s by a couple made wealthy from insurance and meat-packing investments, was truly a showplace in its prime. It cost $450,000 to build, and besides having 54 rooms, featured romantic turrets, tunnels and trapdoors. The Eppersons were noted for generous financial support of the most worthwhile civic and

"Dears, I am so sorry for you. . .
God bless you, you poor darlings. . ."
They smiled at her with shy little baby smiles. . .
They grew faint, fading slowly away
like wreaths of vapour in the frosty air.

E.F. Benson,
"How Fear Departed from the Long Gallery"

cultural efforts, but did something most unusual. They adopted a woman only a few years younger than themselves, a person of great musical ability. Was their intent to insure her of wherewithal for pursuing her talent? The story doesn't say. It says she died at only 47 of supposed complications from routine surgery while both the Eppersons lived into unusually old age.

Upon visiting the house, a group of psychics led by Maurice Schwalm, who has been prominent in the investigations of many Kansas City haunts, felt indications of drama involving a woman. As relayed in Kansas City publications, these included a possible abortion, someone fleeing via ladder, a bad fall down the grandiose staircase, and someone slashing her wrists. One investigator found an entity strongly resentful of intrusion.

Even today, although the Epperson House is a part of the University of Missouri in Kansas City campus, students and staff working in the building have always insisted that they felt an oppressive atmosphere and many reported mildly frightening sights and sounds.

Probably the best testimony of all comes from a university patrolman who was quoted in May 1979 in the *Kansas City Star*. He said that one night after cruising the area, he parked for a short time and suddenly, in the late, quiet hours, was impacted from behind by another vehicle. He heard all the sounds of collision, including broken glass raining down on the parking lot and metal crumpling. When he got out to look there was no other car in sight and no damage to his own, though his neck ached. Closer scrutiny showed that his car had moved about eight inches, leaving skid marks.

On another occasion, he and a fellow officer were doing their usual 2 a.m. walk-through of the building, turning lights on and off to light their way as they went, thus being separated most of the time by the length of long hallways and large rooms. One light would not turn off and just as the officer nearest it commented on the strangeness, the other saw, behind his friend, an arm in a blue sleeve reach out and flip the switch.

"Who turned that off?" the patrolman asked, turning in puzzlement. "I didn't try to tell him then," the other told the *Star's* reporter. "I just promised to explain when we were outside and we got there as fast as we could." It was these two men's problems with their disbelieving colleagues that led to Schwalm's group being invited in. Schwalm said an improvement in atmosphere probably would be noted just because resident spirits had been given an opportunity to express their feelings. This seemed to be the case, at least when the *Star* story appeared.

The Muhlebach Blonde

The young woman who haunted a restaurant in The Radisson Muhlebach Hotel was quite lovely, yet the sight of her caused one new busboy to

So suddenly I flung the door wide on him.
A tongue of fire flashed out
and licked along his upper teeth.
Smoke rolled inside the sockets of his eyes.
Then he came at me with one hand
outstretched, the way he did in life once;
but this time I struck the hand off
brittle on the floor. . .

Robert Frost, "The Witch of Coos"

run out the door never to return. Her presence seemed to set off troublesome activity in the kitchen and elsewhere. She dressed always in blue, in fashions of the 1930s and 1940s and she must have spoken to someone originally, or been known to people who lived or worked at the Muhlebalch. One employee, a tarot card reader, said for a *Star* story of April 1985, that she had seen the entity six times and had communicated with her telepathically. She said this pensive visitor had been an actress who researched her roles by watching people in public places. It had been her misfortune to have an affair with a gangster who killed her, and this put her on an endless search for an earlier lover who had been kind and protective.

Some of the problems the blue lady's appearances seemed to stimulate included unreliable behavior of lights and other electrical equipment and such events as heavy trays of hors d'oeuvres rising off counters and crashing to the floor. One of the cooks told the *Star* he'd never think of spending any time alone in the restaurant.

Kansas City Shorts

Apparitions, strange sounds and erratic stage lights have been reported for years by students and teachers at Loretto School Auditorium, located along the southern edge of town, and some even said they saw the shadow of a hanged nun. In 1979 so many problems occurred with the light panel that psychics were invited in. Their verdict: the spirit of a woman, formerly a top echelon administrator, was disturbed at plays she considered too freethinking for a Catholic private school. This was not nearly as exciting as the previous assumption of a connection with three students who died tragically on stage in 1909 in burning Halloween costumes. But the school was located elsewhere then, so this story was a bit of a stretch.

The Spanish Chapel's ghost, Schwalm suggested to the *Star* reporter, might be 14th-century martyr, Jacques DeMolay, drawn to this location because some of his ashes somehow got incorporated into some of the chapel's art objects. Ron Taggert, senior curator at the gallery, was quoted by the *Star* as saying he had never seen or felt anything eerie or interesting and has always felt annoyed that whatever haunts the chapel ignores him.

Ghosts in Independence

The Vaille Mansion, built in 1881, has no recent accounts of hauntings, according to Terri Baumgardner in the *Star* in 1996, but its reputation was once so ominous that neighbors crossed the street rather than pass in front of it. The ghost, which children said they've seen in windows, was that of Sylvia Vaille, who died only a few years after her husband built the house

As the day of my death draws nearer,
the intense horror that all living flesh feels
toward escaped spirits from beyond the grave
grows more and more powerful.

Rudyard Kipling, "The Phantom Rickshaw"

for her. He was so unwilling to let her go that he buried her on the front lawn in a glass-topped coffin set flush with the ground. Protests of those who lived nearby soon forced him to give his wife a more conventional burial.

ഔ   Also reported in Independence was a jail built in 1859 with one cell so thoroughly haunted that the casual visitor could pick it out. Gay Clemmens, site director, told Baumgardner that when anyone asked him which cell is haunted he invited them to go and see if they can tell him. Seldom is anyone wrong. He says, too, that guards and inmates have reported nausea and chilling in this building, as well as sounds of inexplicable footsteps, growls and gasps. He also described a psychic thrusting an arm into the cell through its bars and his hair then standing up as if from electrical charge.

The cell became haunted, the story goes, in days when a town's main law enforcement officer had his home in the same building as the jail. Marshall Jim Knowles lost his life trying to settle a fight between prisoners with opposing sentiments during the Civil War. Hauck's *National Directory of Haunted Places* says the haunt is possibly a deputy marshall killed in a jailbreak in June of 1866.

The foregoing is only a sample of what could be written about Missouri's metropolitan ghosts. Surely no cities anywhere can claim more variety.

Chapter Ten

Haunted Houses

Though we've already looked at a number of Missouri's haunted houses, the following are in a special class. All of them still exist and most are listed in the *National Directory of Haunted Places*. Three can be toured and one can even be slept in. One is a private home whose present owners say they've never seen, heard or felt anything unusual in it.

The Lemp Mansion

Surprisingly, the 33-room Lemp Mansion on De Menil Place in St. Louis hasn't had its share of attention in the annals of the ghostly, despite *Life Magazine's* 1980 designation. Here's what gives the place such remarkable qualifications. Three members of the Lemp family killed themselves under its roof and a fourth elsewhere. At least one family member died a lingering death there and a favorite and promising Lemp son sickened there of an ailment that would take his life at only age 28. Within the walls of this house, a large and powerful family dwindled to just a few and saw a great fortune lost. The home itself went from being a jewel in the city's crown to ever cheapening apartments and rental rooms. It sold in 1974 for $40,000—less than a modest subdivision home—and was rescued just in time by an

*It's suprising there aren't
more mutually cooperative relationships
between shamans and spirits.*

Colin Watson

enterprising family. Their loving and respectful efforts have almost completely restored it. As it did in its glory, once again the Lemp Mansion has thousands of guests each year, though these guests pay to eat there or to stay in its bed and breakfast rooms.

The house was built in the 1880s for John Adam Lemp, who brought the first lager beer to St. Louis in 1838. He developed the Falstaff line among several others and his son, William, carried the dynasty forward to even greater prominence. The third generation, under the leadership of William Lemp, Jr., brought the business to its peak. Its buildings covered eleven city blocks and the annual income grew to 3.5 million dollars for an output of 500,000 barrels of beer. But "Billy" Lemp apparently destroyed it all through his despair about Prohibition. In 1919, he closed the brewery "to spite the government," according to Jeff Meyer, who wrote about the house and the family for the *Post-Dispatch* in September 1979. William Jr. sold Falstaff to the Griesedieck family for $25,000 and the brewery buildings for eight cents on the dollar to a shoe manufacturer.

This would have been enough to inspire his grandfather's suicide, but that had taken place in 1902 after Frederick's death. William Jr. killed himself in 1922 in the same room by the same means—a small calibre bullet to the heart. Reclusive Charles Lemp committed suicide in the basement of the house, some sources say, after killing his dog, and a sister killed herself in her luxurious home in Hortense Place.

Meyer wrote that in 1979 the atmosphere of the Lemp Mansion was forbidding and sad from outdoors and unnerving inside. Pictures from *Post-Dispatch* photographers reinforced that description, showing dark paneling and windows too clouded with dirt to let in much light.

Dick and Patti Pointer, who bought the house, immediately began clearing the place out to make it a restaurant. With their nine children's help, they reached their goal in less than three years. The first task was carting off debris. For the first seven months they did nothing but haul trash from the place. As they worked, they made time to watch for anything that might have belonged there originally, furniture or pieces of decorative wood. They investigated walls and ceilings added to convert the house for apartments and made many exciting discoveries; they could hardly believe how many of the mansion's beauties had survived its worst days. The Pointers then researched the house exhaustively, looking for pictures that might show them where their findings belonged.

As to feeling the place was haunted: members of the family experienced differing vague to acute discomforts, mainly sensations of being watched and unwelcome. For some, Meyer wrote, it was a daily battle at first, ignoring unearthly presences that "seemed to follow them from one

A house is never silent in darkness

to those who listen intently;

there is a whispering in distant chambers,

an unearthly hand presses the snib of the window,

the latch rises.

Ghosts were created when the first man

woke in the night.

James Matthew Barrie, "The Little Minister"

dark corner of the house to another." An artist brought in to restore a ceiling, knowing nothing of the house's history, fled one day after feeling relentlessly hostile eyes on him for an extended period. He told Pointer, "This place is crazy. You've got a ghost or something here."

Dick Pointer, who had been a paratrooper and felt he was "not scared of anything," admitted that one day while painting in a bathroom, he began to feel someone watching him intently. He said it was "the most terrible sensation you can have. I get goosebumps now, just thinking about it." He turned around and saw nothing, but when it happened again, he said, "I cleaned my brushes and got the Hell out."

The situation was not helped by people from the neighborhood and former renters telling the Pointers weird tales. One aged woman said the Lemps were reputed to keep a retarded child in the attic and people who saw it at windows said it looked like a monkey. The Pointers told each other that such stories were natural for those who had lived for years near a house with such history and appearance.

Meyer's story said a Pointer son, Dick Jr., lived alone in the mansion for four years after the restaurant was in operation, his parents and siblings living nearby, all working together by day. Dick Jr., who insisted he did not believe in ghosts, shared basement quarters with his Doberman, Shadow. Only once did they have an unexplainable experience: awakened by what sounded like a kick to their door, they made a run through the house, but found nothing amiss. Dick Jr. reported no feelings in those years of being observed and resented, and according to one writer, Shadow never displayed any unusual reactions. Another writer mentioned that the dog would not go above the ground floor, possibly referring to another dog.

The Pointer family found that the place's reputation worked for its preservation; neighborhood children did not try to explore it. Only after Meyer's story appeared did the family take time to check out features of the property that had inspired awe in those nearby: an underground pool and dance floor and access to what are called the Cherokee caves. These caverns, named for their location along Cherokee Street, had been a big reason for Lemp's choosing the site; they provided natural refrigeration for storage of his beer.

Today the Lemp Mansion is a beautiful, non-frightening place and the renovation must please its spirits, if any, because nothing really unpleasant happens there. Things have moved about, says Paul Pointer, present owner and operator of the restaurant and bed and breakfast. They've done this both in poltergeist manner and just as apparent misplacements that turn up in remarkable spots. Lights and appliances sometimes behave strangely; doors may be unaccountably locked or unlocked; candles on a mantel once lit

If a house was seated on some melancholy place,
or built in some old romantic manner,
or if any particular accident had happened in it,
such as murder, sudden death or the like. . .
That house had a mark set on it,
and was afterwards esteemed
the habitation of a ghost.

Bourne's Antiquities

themselves and once, while he was in conversation about the Lemp ghosts, a wine glass rose up from a counter and dashed itself on the floor.

Here's a typical little episode from the Lemp Mansion nowadays. An employee saw an elderly man come in and sit down, obviously waiting for service, when the restaurant was not yet open for business. She couldn't figure out where he'd come from, but turned aside for an instant to get him a cup of coffee to make it a little more gracious, telling him he was too early. Turning back around, she saw nobody and he had been too close to her to have got out of the large room that fast.

Another event had a useful outcome; members of the family heard the sound of horse hooves at a side entrance. Nothing was there, of course, but their looking for tracks brought the discovery of a cobbled area lost in grass. This had apparently been laid to ensure a clear place for alighting from carriages; the Pointers used the cobblestone to make a distinctive floor for one of the basement rooms.

Most of what happens Pointer just considers "interesting." For instance, in going through his late father's papers, he found a letter someone had written him when the family first acquired the house. A former tenant described an unusual man seen regularly while the Lemp Mansion served as apartments. He was smaller than average size, always dressed nattily in vintage looking clothing, notable for always having on new looking and wonderfully cared for shoes. He bustled along on business of his own, not returning greetings. Nobody knew who he was or what floor he lived on, but he was seen constantly in the hallways and on nearby streets. Some of the Lemps were small people and most of them dressed very well indeed.

Paul Pointer had never discussed this letter with anyone who was writing about the house. In fact, he had almost forgotten it until someone came in and told him essentially the same story. This person, however, had lived at the Lemp Mansion at another time entirely from that of the letter writer. Pointer says he went home and dug out the letter and was amazed to see how perfectly the two accounts matched.

The story of the Lemp Mansion is told in the book titled *Lemp: A Haunting History*, by Stephen P. Walker.

Ravenswood

This declining mansion seems to house a spirit who still cherishes her privacy and feels possessive about her clothing. We're told that on the day after Nadine Leonard's death, the door of her bedroom was locked and remained so for some days, defying all non-damaging ways to get it open. Fortunately for the door, it didn't have to be pried open. It seemingly un-

. . .They sometimes

come down the stairs at night

and stand perplexed behind the door

and headboard of the bed,

brushing their chalky skull with chalky fingers

that sounds like the dry rattling of a shutter. . .

Robert Frost, "The Witch of Coos"

locked itself just in time to avoid force. In another instance, when Nadine's wardrobe was being reorganized for display and left lying about overnight in a rather disorderly manner, an employee came in the next morning and found her clothing all neatly folded and returned to storage.

Ravenswood is in Cooper County near Boonville and is open for tours. It was built in 1880 of brick manufactured on site, and the property includes 2,000 acres of land owned continuously by one family from 1825 to the present. The house was constructed for Charles E. Leonard, a Union captain, and his bride, Nadine Nelson, "the belle of Boonville," the beautiful and pampered daughter of one of the area's first millionaires. A showcase of the technology of its time, Ravenswood had more than 30 rooms, running water, gas lights, a fireplace in each room, elaborate plasterwork ceilings and a greenhouse. Nadine's initials as a married woman are even etched into the front door's frosted glass.

The newlyweds traveled the world, she gathering lovely furnishings and ornaments for Ravenswood and he adding to his famous herd of shorthorns, the first of their breed imported west of the Mississippi. The couple returned with their treasures and made their home one of the state's most choice sites for entertaining. Ravenswood was famous for its "fairy-lighted lawn parties" with a permanently standing dance pavilion. Parties of more than 100 people were common.

Nadine's sister, Maggie, was married to Lon Stephens, Missouri's governor. They gave Nadine's gatherings special status, attracting state celebrities of the era to eat, sleep and dance.

Staff capabilities were demonstrated when a certain dance ended and 100 or so guests started home, only to come trooping back because a stream was up and they couldn't cross. Nadine, who was preparing for bed, put her dress back on, told the musicians to continue playing until daylight, and with her husband she resumed the dance. At dawn a hearty country breakfast was served to all guests and by the time that was over, the water had subsided.

One little detail could have caused marital problems that would inspire ghost stories. Despite all its attractions, Nadine didn't really like Ravenswood much. (One of her complaints: "Must the peacocks scream *all* the time?") She preferred the town house her father had given her, because she relished the social activity of Boonville and didn't like the constant carriage trips back and forth to Ravenswood. Charles apparently adapted to this without annoyance, commuting between the farm and the townhouse.

At its peak, the house was full of Venetian glass and Italian tapestries, and it still has its suit of armor in the hall, its family portraits by George Caleb Bingham, an impressive library, and many of Nadine's exquisite

It is important to note
that it is the malignant ghosts,
chiefly those who have been involved
in murder or other evil acts,
which especially linger
around the scene of their earthly activities.

New International Encyclopedia, 1903

dresses. These include her tiny ivory satin wedding gown, and a gauzy navy and grey creation made for Grover Cleveland's inauguration. She had at least one Worth gown, a great status symbol of wealthy women of her time, and a multitude of dainty long-sleeved little tops, short and tightly fitted, decorated with painstaking needlework—embroidery, appliqué, braiding and fringe. These are lined throughout with delicate boning that would make slumping impossible. They were hand sewn for her in Europe from measurements given on her wedding trip, ordered as she desired new ones.

Ravenswood's haunting reports have been the usual passersby accounts of floating lights and of music wafting faintly from the lawn, as well as many a visitor's firm statement: "you can feel her there...not offended that we're in her house, just there." Guests and family members have reported a large metal disc music box in an upstairs hall spontaneously playing, usually after midnight. Family members also have reported hearing downstairs crashes so frightening they never dreamed of going to investigate until daylight, and then, without exception, finding no hint of what it could have been. One description: "...like someone down there with a sledge hammer just taking things apart. It lasted for fifteen minutes...left no trace."

Ravenswood has only one tragedy to foster ghosts. Nadine lived to be past 90, but her one son, Nelson, collector of the library, died at the estate's entrance when his car slipped out of gear and crushed him against the gate he was opening.

Longview

Near Kansas City, at Holt's Summit, is an estate that any horse-loving spirit would understandably be reluctant to leave. It was, when lumber tycoon A.C. Long established it in 1911, called "horse heaven" and "American Versailles"—an international wonder of the equine world. The estate contained seven miles of bridle path and driving roads, accompanied by so much white fence that Longview had a team of men who did nothing but keep its paint pristine. On its 1,780 acres stood a literal village of stucco buildings with red tile roofs. Besides the 50-room family home, there were dozens of buildings to house staff, different kinds of animals, farm equipment and Longview's veterinary hospital. Long also built a chapel with a school in the basement for the employees' 60 children. He even insisted that the farm have its own water tower to provide filtered water for all souls, human and otherwise. Where loveliness was concerned, there was a 20-acre artificial lake and everywhere were flowers, in beds and borders and pergolas, in arbors and sunken gardens.

At its peak, Longview had 400 employees but the family was only four, Long and his Quaker wife and two daughters. Of these two girls, the younger,

The whispering got even louder

and I could detect anger in the voice,

but I couldn't understand the words.

Then I heard another voice from off to my right.

It said, "Speak to her in English.

She isn't ignoring you,

she just doesn't understand!"

Lorna

Loula, became world renowned as an incredible winner at horse shows, both riding as a young person and driving in her maturity. She competed from the age of 15 to her early 80s winning hundreds of ribbons and trophies, as well as thousands in cash prizes. A memorable characterization of life at Longview came when she wrote "My father never refused to buy any horse I wanted, and I wanted many of them."

For horses were what Longview was really about, dozens and dozens of them, though it had all kinds of animals and the crops to provide their food. Long imported a Scottish driving ace to train the harness horses and John Hook of Mexico, Mo., the country's top trainer then, to breed Saddlebreds and prepare them for exhibition. These three men assembled what was called "the biggest saddlebred nursery in the world," made up of the finest mares that could be bought and three great stallions, My Major Dare, Easter Cloud and Independence Chief.

Longview's ghost stories reflect the idyllic life of Loula Long Combs who operated the property as a mature married woman after her father's death. She wrote of how a ride or drive could lift her spirits instantly if she was tired or troubled and she boldly admitted praying for her horses if they were hurt or ill. People who worked at Longview have told how she drifted about with or without horses, accompanied by a cloud of dogs and other pets—including a pig—how she planned and executed charity shows in which only Longview's many horses performed. They recount her kindness to all of them and her special interest in their children.

Predictably, what the ghostly Loula is said to do today is allow hoof-beats to be heard as she rides or drives by, to let people glimpse her sometimes in the half-dark of the indoor arena, or just see a sparkle of light flying off silvery-spoked wheels. Employees are reluctant to enter this place alone, some writers say. The only even mildly pettish thing that has ever been implied Loula might have done was once when the family home was open for tour, people working there reported that her bed was in disarray each morning, as if it had been slept in.

Longview's acreage is greatly reduced now, partly flooded by the Corps of Engineers, partly sold off or given away by Loula and her sister Sally in their final years. Longview Community College occupies land they donated for the purpose. Part of the farm has become a luxury subdivision with some of the horse facilities used by a local riding club. Other portions are utilized by horse people who travel from all over the state and beyond to enjoy the rolling expanses for cross-country riding.

Loula Long Combs' autobiography, *My Revelation*, might encourage us to imagine her there, driving her beloved hackney, Revelation, over familiar paths. After recording her love and appreciation for the place and

Total annihilation is impossible. . .
nothing perishes. Neither a body nor a thought
can drop out of the universe. . .

Maurice Maeterlinck, "Death"

the family, staff and creatures—Mrs. Combs shared her own conviction that "...one day we will meet again those animal friends...by crystal streams in green pastures of heavenly beauty. A dream you say? Who knows?"

Lilac Hill

"We've never really been afraid, because we know if there is such a thing it can't hurt you, but gee whiz, it's just really weird." That's what Joe Jeff Davis told a *St. Louis Post-Dispatch* reporter in 1977, while his family still owned and lived in Lilac Hill, near Fayette in Howard County. This three-story classic Federalist house, built in 1832-33 by A.W. Morrison, sits amid 365 acres on a hill overlooking miles of hills, woodlands and farms. It is one of the oldest houses in Central Missouri, built by slave labor of handmade brick, its parts fitted together with pegs of wood and iron, its walls two feet thick in some places. The estate's name came from hundreds of lilac bushes which once surrounded the house and Marsha Davis says that when she lived there, more than 50 remained, white and French, as well as the old fashioned kind. She assumes that in the Morrisons' days, there may have been many other varieties.

Lilac Hill is listed on the *National Registry of Historic Sites*, the *Missouri Historic Sites Catalog* and the *National Directory of Haunted Sites*. The Morrison family occupied it until 1952 when the last descendant died there at the age of 50. Between then and 1974, when the Davises moved in, four families lived at Lilac Hill and so far as the Davises could learn, none of them complained of hauntings.

The couple and their five children experienced the sound of firm footsteps in the night, sometimes coming into the parents' bedroom, rustling paper, muffled screaming that once went on for two hours in overhead space that had once been the loom room where some female slaves worked, dragging sounds from upstairs for four hours, weeping that seemed to come from a corner of the parents' bedroom, flashing lights, foul odors, cold drafts, the sound of arguments, and unusual behavior from their dog.

Some of these happenings were very perplexing, especially the prolonged weeping. When it began, the Davises first thought one of the children was having a nightmare, but checked and found them all sleeping peacefully. Then Davis went outdoors to look, thinking there could have been a car wreck or some other sort of accident. During an equally long session of overhead noises, they seriously thought of going to a motel for the night, but decided to remain. They had a great deal invested in the place and loved it. It was exactly the right size for their family. Nothing personally threatening had happened. The closest to that was when one son felt so certain someone was behind him on the stairs that he ran into his

And there are those
whose lips quiver and hands tremble
as they carefully measure their words
and their thoughts to recall and reveal
most unsettling and unexplainable encounters
with the unknown.

Anonymous

room and out the window and down the slanting roof to the ground. "It wasn't far," his mother said, "and he was fit and athletic. That was the closest we came to actual danger."

The couple told a newspaper reporter in 1987 of a son-in-law who was a total disbeliever, but on one visit wound up on the family room floor with a blanket over his head because something walked around his bed. Then he felt the weight of someone sitting down on it and a woman's voice said, "Don't worry. I'll only be here a little while."

No one in the family doubted him, because the parents once had a similar experience. Davis had gone on to bed while Marsha stayed up a bit longer to take clothes from the dryer and fold them. When she came into the bedroom, he asked if she'd come in earlier and laid down. He said somebody had entered the room, walked around to her side of the bed and he'd felt the weight and turned over to put his arm around her and nothing was there. He thought she'd just gotten up again.

Because the Davises talked freely to the media about their house, a group of psychics from Kansas City asked for permission to visit and when they did, reported finding the main entity there was a woman named Minerva, known to the staff and neighbors as "Miss Minnie," and that she still considered herself mistress of the house. This could have been either the last resident or the builder's wife. The latter lady's gravestone had been displaced by some previous tenant who cleared space and put outbuildings where the family cemetery stood. The stone said she was born in 1808 and died in 1858.

The psychics, headed by Maurice Schwalm, also mentioned that activity is often higher in a house where children live, and it did abate for the Davises when two of their children left home and Mr. Davis' mother, in her 80s, came to live with them. The next family to occupy the house declared they saw and heard nothing, but the next, David and Joanie Wells, who had no children, saw things the Davises did not see as well as many of the same manifestations. These included crashes similar to a quantity of plaster falling or a chandelier, after which they could find nothing out of order. At times they heard male and female voices in urgent conversation. Their Cocker Spaniel, Buffy, sometimes chased things nobody could see.

The next and present dwellers, Ken and Carol Staten, declare that they have seen, heard and felt nothing unusual at Lilac Hill. An air force retiree, he says it is a great improvement over living in Washington, D.C., where they were before. They had wanted to get away from the city and bought the house after looking at it for less than an hour. "The acreage is just what I wanted for raising cattle," he says, "and the house is just what my wife wanted." He is a member of the Fayette Area Heritage Association.

*In an old house
there is always listening
and more is heard
than is spoken*

T.S. Eliot

The James Family Farm

How could the family farm of Jesse James near Kearney in Clay County not be haunted? There Zerelda Cole James Sims Samuel lived with three different husbands and bore seven children. There she saw her ten-year-old Archie killed by Pinkerton detectives and lost her own right hand. On that property she also saw her husband tortured, never to recover. There she endured suspense about the well-being of her famous two older sons and gave them refuge when they needed it. There she fended off their foes, legal and illegal. Most of all, on this farm she guarded the body of her son, Jesse, after his murder, with a grave dug extra deep and in sight of her bedroom window. She spent most of her widowhood on the farm, some-times alone except for servants, as did her daughter-in-law, Annie Ralston James. Annie and Frank James' son, Robert, also spent his later life there, sometimes alone, sometimes with a wife. In addition to the emotional moun-tain these people would have created on the property, there were the joys and despairs of siblings of the famous "boys" and a family of slaves that remained on for generations as paid servants.

The James family farm has always had a reputation for being haunted, with the reports one would expect: moving lights in and around the house, sounds of pounding hooves, muffled shouts, shots and wailings. Surpris-ingly little has been written about these haunts, in comparison to all that was written about the brothers' exploits while they were alive. In January 1982, the *Kansas City Star* reviewed an overnight vigil in the house to mark the 100th anniversary of the death of Archie Samuel, the only person to ever die violently in the house. This came about when detectives, hoping to flush out Jesse and Frank whom the family has always maintained were not even there, threw some sort of incendiary device into the house. The im-pact or shrapnel killed young Archie and damaged Zerelda's arm so badly that her hand and forearm had to be amputated. Some sources say this was done without anesthesia and there in the house, by her own husband, a physician. Officers of the James-Younger gang, which documents family his-tory and helps maintain the house, believe another doctor may have been brought in for the purpose.

Despite all the psychic drama this event could have produced on its 100th anniversary, the men in the house that night felt nothing but a cold draft, which Milton F. Perry, curator of the museum, laughed about as typi-cal of any aged and unheated cabin in January. The vigil keepers, two men from Chicago, with *Kansas City Star* writer D. P. Breckenridge, said they spent most of their time huddled around the fireplace, warmly dressed.

There are in this land, ghosts. . .

the terrible ghosts of women

who have died in child-bed. . .

wander the pathways at dusk. . .

their feet are turned backward

that all sober men may recognize them.

There are ghosts of little children. . .

who wail under the stars

or catch women by the wrist

and beg to be taken up and carried.

Rudyard Kipling, "My Own True Ghost Story"

However, people who work in the house, volunteers and employees who take care of its upkeep and exhibits, have had more interesting experiences. These are few and mild, considering all that happened there and those who tell them are the first to admit being so totally saturated in the history of the family that they hardly regard the Jameses as gone.

They laugh about a summer day when several people together were rehanging freshly laundered curtains. They began feeling apprehensive as a sudden thunderstorm came up. When it sent drafts into the house that violently slammed several outer and inner doors in quick succession, they all fled, not exchanging a word or a look first.

A less explainable happening: the framed picture of Jesse on his grey horse Stonewall has never hung straight, no matter what new hangers and adjustments were tried. When it went away for reframing, and to be treated for museum preservation, everyone assumed that problem would be solved, but the picture still hangs at the same angle as before.

Reports continue of lights seen in the house when it is locked up and of movements to which its monitoring system does not react. Another type of security system activates by itself several times a year, never in daytime, never earlier than midnight.

At times, the feelings of presence here are so intense that many guides prefer not to be alone in the house. A sensation several have shared is the feeling that someone else has entered the room, after a tour group is admitted, even though the door is always locked to prevent anyone's coming in and wandering around unsupervised.

In the "death room" which displays the feather duster, picture and stool that saw Jesse's death, as well as one of his coffin lids, light bulbs burn out at a remarkable rate, far faster than anywhere else in the house. Staff members all try to avoid being the person who puts in the new bulbs.

One staff member says she has more than once, on foggy mornings, when sound carries strangely anyhow, heard the hushed voices of men from woods fairly near the house, and restless movements of horses, which reminds her that sometimes Frank and James waited there for a sign that it was safe to come on to the house. Later in the day, with others, when she goes to look, this worker never finds any tracks.

A guide, taking a group of people through at night in a tour held in connection with some special event, was startled to hear overhead a frantic scrabbling, as of some animal like a raccoon in the attic. Almost immediately, from two sides of the room, came loud, substantial rustlings in the leaves outside, reminding her of the fact that the Pinkertons surrounded the house on the night of their attack. A wild animal sheltering in the attic might well have heard their approach and taken flight.

Some say no evil thing that walks by night

In fog or fire, by lake or moorish fen,

Blue meagre hag, or stubborn unlaid ghost

That breaks his magic chains at curfew time,

...Hath hurtful power o'er true virginity.

Milton, "Comus"

Some of the staff were experimenting one day with grave witching, a variation on water witching where two copper wires replace the willow wands. These are commonly used by genealogists and others looking for grave sites, the idea being that the wires' L-shaped ends will move together when held over soil that has been disturbed to a depth of more than six inches. Over Jesse James' twice dug-up gravesite, they said, these wire ends first crossed each other, then vibrated so strongly that the operator dropped them.

Just across the road from the James farmstead is a nice antebellum house called Claybrook, which was the home of Jesse and Zee James' daughter, Mary, and her husband, Henry Barr. This house, where their baby daughter, Henrietta died, and a later resident hanged himself, is said to be haunted by a child's cries, by the sound of someone clearing his throat, by footsteps going up and down the divided front staircase and by the sound of a ball bouncing down those stairs. On one occasion, staff members say, a female member of a tour group came running down the stairs, white faced, and raced out to her car and away, with no explanation to anyone, ever. Today Claybrook, fully restored, is maintained by the county as a historic site.

Despite the causes for their fame, all biographers agree that the James family maintained a loyal and loving closeness. They would probably agree with Mark Twain, "The spirits of the dead hallow a house..."

Chapter Eleven

Haunted Horses & Other Creatures

Since Missouri is fifth in horse population among all the states, it's only natural that they should far outnumber other creatures in our ghost stories. Also, Vance Randolph and other folklorists tell us that these animals will show us ghosts, if any are near. We need only look straight out between a horse's ears. Even horsepeople too young to ever have heard this will jokingly attribute to horses an ability to sense ghosts, or to think they do. The language of horse people is full of it. "She's young and spooky, yet," they'll say of an animal who has not yet learned to take the unexpected in stride. "Oh...spooky looking!" they'll say of an area containing sights that might alarm horses.

But this can be complicated. I have a friend who warned me that one end of her ring is haunted, "Every horse who comes here wants to shy in that spot, even when they've not seen another one do it..." Perhaps one horse did experience a legitimate fright there and exuded something that stays around, like what bloodhounds pick up on? Maybe other horses notice and add their own fear until the place is heavy with warning.

And still of a winter's night, they say,

when the wind is in the trees,

when the moon is a ghostly galleon,

tossed upon cloudy seas....

the highwayman comes riding, riding, riding;

the highway man comes riding...

Alfred Noyes, "The Highwayman"

Or, maybe they really do see apparitions of the traditionally attired variety, for horses certainly have an almost universal aversion to moving white objects. A piece of paper blowing across the road, a plastic bag caught in a bush, a bedsheet flapping on a nearby clothesline—it takes most horses years of safely passing such things before they can ignore them. Some never can. For this reason, owners often make a point of keeping live white things around them, barn cats or dogs of some large European guard breeds. A horse who lives with white things moving around in his space all the time is less likely to shy or bolt when he meets one on the road. A friend of mine even has a big barn cat who is named, appropriately, White Thing. So, on to stories of horses and white things, visible or not.

The Horse Who Came to Church

Probably our best horse ghost story came from an event at a little settlement named Sand Springs, which was between Rolla and Springfield, not far from Roubidoux Creek. During the Civil War, this church had a minister named Maupins who was not very well liked. His morals regarding women were in question, and he was rumored to ride with the Jayhawkers, who just before the Border Wars with Kansas, terrorized people loyal to the South. But having any kind of a minister was a luxury in those days, and people tried to overlook the fact that Maupins often devoted his sermons to rebel bashing. A Confederate officer, Charles Potter, retired because of war injuries, lived in the area and was not alone in wishing Maupins were elsewhere. Finally he told friends that he would face the man down in the church and send him packing.

When Potter appeared he was in uniform and on his fine black horse, an animal who had shared his war experience and had injuries of its own. They came down the aisle and stopped in front of the pulpit, but just as Potter began his speech, someone shot him in the back. The shot came from outside, through an open window.

Potter slumped in his saddle and then slid to the floor. The horse bent its head to him, hesitated for a moment, and then turned and walked slowly back down the aisle, out the door and across the porch, his shod feet very loud in the silence. Maupins, probably prepared for what had happened, knelt and commanded the congregation to join him in praying for their safety. This enabled the shooter to escape.

Haunted Heartland and Judge Moore both extended this story elaborately, going into the matter of who the shooter was, her relationship with the preacher, and what became of them all. For our purposes, the main details are that forever after this night, many people claimed to hear a shod horse's hooves on the wooden floor whenever they were in the church, day

If a step should sound
or a word be spoken
Would a ghost not rise
at the stranger's hand?

Algernon Swinburne

or night, at services or for some other reason. In time, the building deteriorated beyond use as a church, but was utilized by travelers who needed shelter. It was these people who gave the story the most credibility, because they knew nothing of what had happened earlier. Wayfaring strangers frequently asked local people about the horse who lived in the old church.

A determined debunker might point out that the story tells us nothing about when the horse himself became capable of ghosthood. They might ask whether this is a case of a live animal being a haunt, or what. Regardless, the tale has found its way into many books for more than a century after it was said to have happened.

Haunted Homecoming

In the 1960s a group of Lebanon high school students made a collection of ghost stories and other folklore. From this material, for several years, they produced a magazine named *Bittersweet*. Here's the group's best ghost story in which a horse participated.

Near Plad, around 1910, lived a farm family with a son named Lowell who worked elsewhere, but usually joined them on weekends. This Saturday he had not appeared, but no one was concerned, for he was a reliable and capable person. They did their usual hard day's work, which for his sister, whom we'll call Mary, included preparing Lowell's bedroom. She went to bed early and was too drowsy to more than note with relief the sound of his horse trotting up the lane and across the yard to the porch.

Familiar sounds brought her wide-awake, however. She heard her brother dismount onto the wooden porch, his spurs jingling, heard him speak softly to the horse as he untacked it and leaned his saddle against the wall. As usual, he gave the horse a little slap and a word or two to send it off to graze, and he came into Mary's room and paused by her bed. Not turning over to look at him, because it was too dark to see, she said, "Go on up, Lowell. Your bed's ready."

He didn't answer, just climbed the stairs accompanied by the sound of his spurs, went into his room and closed the door. Next morning when Lowell didn't come down to breakfast, someone went to rouse him and found the bed untouched. Mary's story was checked out: no horse in the yard, no hoofprints anywhere, no saddle on the porch. The family spent an anxious day, believing, in the attitude of the time, that Lowell had made his final homecoming. In late afternoon, however, he rode in, hale and hearty, having been delayed by pleasant events. All were left to wonder, who, if anyone, had spent the night in their house!

Afrits are spirits that emerge from a murdered
person's blood wherever it falls on the ground.
The afrit materializes to retaliate the murder
and is often quite frightening.
To eliminate his pesky pranks,
you have to drive a new nail into the ground
where the victim was slain.

Anonymous

A White Hat Guy

A nother of the Lebanon students' horse stories takes place at Oak Grove School, site of the tale given earlier here about the grinning ghost who could be seen only from outdoors, and who inspired a group of horses to bolt en masse. Quite a few years later a young man returning from a rather distant party, stopped under the largest of the oak trees that gave the school its name. He needed to rest his fancy new horse—equivalent in his era to a sports car in ours—and perhaps he was thinking about what a sensation he'd been among his friends with this enviable horse and his big white western hat.

Rustlings drew the rider's eyes up and he saw someone sitting on a branch just above his head. The man wore a silly expression, suggesting that he might be drunk, which could mean he should be helped down from the tree and pointed toward home. He did not respond to friendly conversation however, and at some point the party-goer decided that he, himself, might be the one in danger. The story doesn't tell us exactly what led up to it, but in panic he fired his gun. The man on the branch leaned down, plucked off the white hat and flung it down in front of the horse, who reared in panic and set out at a dead run.

No doubt the rider urged him on, for the animal was badly spent when they got home, and his owner was in worse condition emotionally. He jumped off his mare, left his expensive status symbol standing in its sweat and tack, and ran upstairs to bed, spurs and all. His family found him the next morning with his head still under the covers. We might like to know the horse's fate, but like so many ghost stories, this one ends where it ends.

A Horseman Who Wasn't

A nother story from the Lebanon students tells of two young brothers who had walked five miles one afternoon to attend evening church services. When they got there, they found the meeting had been canceled. Tired and disappointed, they started the long trek back home. Twilight found them still trudging along a narrow country road. When they heard a horse coming fast from ahead of them, they separated, one to each side of the road to give the rider plenty of room to pass. They heard and felt all they'd expect, clicking of bridle rings, creak of leather, rush of air. But there was no horse, no rider. The boys stood staring at each other as the hoof-beats faded away and then, with no need to consult one another, started running as hard as they could. Their fatigue was soon forgotten—they only hoped the ghostly horseman would not turn around and pass them again. The story says they didn't stop running until they were in sight of home.

*Pooka ghosts often take the form
of a black animal or half-animal.
If you're being haunted by a Pooka,
and he likes you, he'll teach you
to understand animal speech
and protect you from evil spirits.*

Anonymous

Colts & Butternut

More than one anthology tells of a strange horseman who haunted a certain portion of a road near Bolivar. Residents of the area thought he was the spirit of a horse thief unknown locally who had been hanged and hastily buried nearby. However, this was one of those apparitions appearing so real that on encountering him, nobody thought anything about it until later. Anyone could see that he wore two good Colt revolvers, that his boots were battered but had been fine ones, that his trousers were of the sturdy butternut fabric many a rebel soldier took years to wear out after the war. This man rode a strong and handsome horse.

Most who saw this rider considered him just a traveler who did not reply to their greeting or move aside politely to let them pass. And strangely, no one's horse ever greeted his or even looked at it. A few claimed to have been chased by this horseman when they met him at night. One man claimed to have been shot in the back by him and he displayed bullet holes in his shirt and jacket, but there were no holes in his flesh. It was also whispered that someone in the area knew the horse thief, because flowers were sometimes placed on his unmarked grave.

Randolph's Spin on Horses

Here are some of the horses Vance Randolph told of, in his book *Ozark Magic and Folklore:*

    ∞   A tall white horse ridden by a military man appeared silently at the gate of a farm house where a large family had gathered at the bedside of their aged patriarch. Several men, sitting outdoors, greeted the newcomer, supposing he was another relative. However, in only a moment they recognized something eerie about the pair, and watched them both disappear just as someone came to the door to announce the elderly man's passing.

    ∞   Near Dead Man's Pond, a few miles from Reeds Spring, a young man named Palmer E. Sharp had a strange experience with an "empty" horse. He had taken the animal for a young lady to ride to a dance he'd invited her to. Now, having delivered her safely to her parents, he was homeward bound himself, when he noticed the extra horse was lagging in an odd way. Scolding it and jerking the lead did no good, and when he looked back, he saw, momentarily, a man sitting on its back. The image faded so quickly he said he could not have told any detail of how the phantom looked or what he wore.

Marley's face. . .had a dismal light about it,
like a bad lobster in a dark cellar.
It was not angry or ferocious,
but looked at Scrooge as Marley used to look:
with ghostly spectacles turned up
upon its ghostly forehead.

Charles Dickens, "A Christmas Carol"

The body of water Palmer was near had a reputation for being haunted, since once in a drought, its low water level exposed some human bones. The late May Kennedy McCord, a well-known Missouri radio personality of the 1940s, was native to the Reeds Spring area. She openly said that she'd not think of going near that particular pond at night.

A Haunted Horse Farm

A few miles north of Columbia is a 100-acre farm called Skyrim, which has for decades teemed with horses and horse activity. On this farm, Alice Thompson and her late partner, Dick Cook, raised, trained and bred a quantity of American Saddlebreds and coached show horse exhibitors. Many of their horses have been outstanding in the ring and their favorite stallion, Skyrim's Bourbon Stonewall, was for many years one of the highest ranking of his breed in the United States for begetting show winners.

Alice's parents, John G. and Mona Neihardt owned this property. His career included teaching at the University of Missouri-Columbia and selling many thousands of books, much of it poetry. He was also named Nebraska's poet laureate. Being of mystic bent himself, Neihardt was fascinated with the Sioux religion and their spiritual leaders. His most famous book, *Black Elk Speaks*, was called "the bible of the young" in the 1960s. In fact, it was Nebraska University Press' biggest seller of all time.

While he lived at Skyrim, Neihardt led a group of people who shared his interests in a series of "psi" experiments. Several of these people taught at the university. Some were local writers. They worked in the scientific way, doing all experiments as a group, repeatedly, and documenting each event carefully. The group did successful telekinesis, apportation, and various types of channeling.

During this period, and since, a number of remarkable things have happened at the farm. Maurice Schwalm, psychical investigator from Kansas City, was present in 1984 and wrote about the gathering for a regional Mensa publication. He said people from several states attended and that results were some of the most powerful and unique he had ever seen. One manifestation was a sound like a locomotive moving through the house, producing an almost unbearable noise and vibration.

Neihardt's granddaughter, Lynn Frazee, grew up at Skyrim as noted before. Lynn says all of the paranormal activities she experienced there were pleasant. For example, when her grandmother died suddenly from the effects of a traffic accident, the children were devastated, for she had been a vital and loving anchor in their lives. Lynn's bedtime was always enhanced by hearing the small sounds her grandmother made in nearby rooms as she moved about barefoot, in a rustling long robe. When Mrs. Neihardt ended

Spooks are quiet, harmless,
and rather timid ghosts
that often move in and out
of the bodies of living people.

Anonymous

her evening's reading, she went to check the furnace, then performed her last act before bed—a kiss for each sleeping grandchild. Lynn usually managed to stay awake until this was done.

Lynn says that for a few weeks after her grandmother's death, while Lynn and her sister were trying very hard to adjust to this big change in their lives, the soothing sounds continued each night as usual, and kisses were delivered on schedule. "They felt like a bubble breaking against my skin," Lynn remembers.

Many of the unusual things that happened at Skyrim, however, centered on the horses. An aroma that Alice called "the sweet burning" heralded both good and bad events pertaining to the animals. In an interview for *Saddle & Bridle* magazine, Alice described this scent as both pleasant, like fresh plant tissue, and unpleasant, like decayed organic material, with an element of ashes and scorching. She and Dick became so accustomed to it that if either smelled it anywhere on the place, they would seek out the other to report it, so they could be prepared for something to happen. If they were together, they would look at each other and one would say, "Yes, there it is again."

Once following the sweet burning, a fine mare bred to their great stallion delivered a lovely foal and seemed to be doing fine, but in a few hours began hemorrhaging. Before they could call the doctor, he drove up, saying, "I just felt like checking the mare again before going home." Thus, he was there to give what help he could, and though the new mother died, her owners were spared the pain of wondering if prompt medical attention might have saved her.

In another event, a foal was born during a thunderstorm and was injured before he was found. The horse remained accident- and illness-prone throughout his life. But Alice said his spirit was so optimistic and joyous in spite of all he went through—so affectionate and trusting in spite of all the things they had to do to try to help him—that it was a privilege to have him around. She said it was as if the sweet burning announced the arrival of a blessing, something endlessly inspiring and touching.

Dogs & Other Critters

Considering how humans bond with their dogs and cats, we might expect to find endless stories of pets who seem to return from the other side to protect, comfort or warn those they loved. We all know, of course, that cats see ghosts. Who has not felt a little chill to see demure Fluff staring intently at something in midair? Sometimes we might detect a dangling spider, or an out-of-season mosquito, but usually we see nothing and can only take comfort in the fact that the cat soon goes cozily back to sleep.

Deep love endures to the end
And far past the end.
If this is my end, I am not afraid.
I am not lonely. I am still yours.

Robinson Jeffers, "The Housedog's Grave"

Most of the animal stories Vance Randolph recorded were unpleasant ones. He told of a group of ghostly pigs who guarded the grave of their owner, who had been buried with all of her jewelry on. In another story, the remains of a long-gone slaughterhouse near Southwest City still resound with the despairing and agonized voices of cows and pigs. In yet another, a phantom fox would appear that hounds would chase until they were exhausted and then the phantom fox would turn into a white and black "feist" dog (an Ozarks term for a playful little mixed-breed dog with no particular talent, good for nothing but "feisting around with the kids").

Randolph's dogs were usually big and black, and were often headless. They were reported by hunters and farmers harassing livestock or game and bullets passed through them with no effect. Some war veterans told Randolph of a large black dog who appeared to their group before any battle in which one or more of them would die.

Night travelers were often frightened by the sudden appearance of these hellish-looking black hounds who accosted them and spooked their horses. One doctor, however, had a different experience. In a certain area, he was always joined by a big black dog who loped companionably along beside him for a mile or so, then stopped and turned back. The doctor didn't know who the dog belonged to, but considered it a nice animal. Surprisingly, his horse was not disturbed when it appeared. Once, as he forded a shallow stream, the doctor happened to look to the side and notice that the friendly dog was neither wading or swimming, but was running on the water's surface.

    ℐ   Another doctor, this one in St. Louis, claimed to have been helped by two ghostly dogs. *Historic Haunted America* reported that Dr. John J. O'Brien had a very sick patient he felt compelled to see again before he himself went to bed. However, it was a night of blinding, blizzardy snow and he soon realized he had no chance at all of finding his destination, in a part of town without streetlights. He wasn't sure he could even find his own house if he tried to! His reliable horse, for the first time in its life, registered strong resentment against his guidance. Then, in the swirling white, the doctor became dimly aware of two huge mastiffs joining them from the front. They took up positions on each side of the horse and led it through the snow to the street the doctor needed.

He meant to relate this stunning event as soon as he got into the house, but his patient was so ill he had to work steadily with her. By the time he left, the snow had stopped and light was breaking. As a member of the patient's family brought his horse around, the doctor finally got to ask, "Who do those mastiffs belong to? I never saw them around here before."

Ghost:

A disembodied spirit.

The soul or spirit as the principle of life.

The immaterial part of man associated with feeling,
thought and moral action.

The soul of a deceased person inhabiting the world.

A good or evil being. The soul of a person
appearing in visible form or otherwise
making its presence known to humans.

D.W. Waldron

The resident shook his head, saying he didn't know of any dogs of that description. Subsequent visits to the neighborhood failed to shed any light on this mystery.

    ⅌   And now for a dog story from our own time: While the Davis family lived at Lilac Hill, they had a large and much loved German Shepherd named Bruce. Having lived with the Davises since puppyhood, Bruce was devoted to their children—jealously keeping strange people away, putting his body between them and anything he considered possibly dangerous.

Bruce slept mainly on the porch, except during bad weather and times when the children brought him in to play. However, he occasionally scratched urgently on the door to get in and then stayed as close as he could to the family. Bruce was far too polite and well trained to ever get up on furniture, but one day Marsha Davis says she heard strange, distressed sounds coming from a room that was typically not used. It contained a tall old bedstead and matching furniture, which had been in the house when they moved in. The room also retained its original fragile antique velvet bedspread and draperies.

Mrs. Davis did not associate the sounds with Bruce, being so different from anything she'd ever heard from him before. But the sounds were not a part of the ghostly repertoire she was accustomed to, so she went to look. As she opened the door, there was the faultless dog, in the center of the bed, with the priceless old spread wadded into a shredded pile under him.

"He was glassy-eyed, like in shock," she said, "and there was jellyish green slime all over everything. We just threw the bedspread away. Poor Bruce. He wasn't himself for half an hour or so. Then he seemed perfectly all right."

A veterinarian said the only logical explanation she could hazard was that Bruce had eaten something toxic that made him deathly sick, but that he managed to free himself of. She said drinking antifreeze would produce green vomit, but a dog would not survive it. She could not think of anything that would produce gelatinous vomit with no identifiable body or plant parts in it. Another doctor found it quite unusual for a mature dog to eat something strange and for a well-loved, trusting dog to go off alone with his problem, rather than to someone he knew would help him if they could.

She also thought it strange that a dog in extremity would take the trouble to climb up on a high bed where it had never been before. So perhaps we can wonder, with the Davises, if Bruce chased something into that room and had some sort of confrontation with an otherworldly presence. His successor at Lilac Hill, as we've noted, was often seen in wild pursuit of something that no one could see.

After his dramatic experience atop the high bed, Bruce lived on at Lilac Hill with his family and moved with them to a new home where he died when he was almost 15—as devoted as ever. Perhaps Sir Oliver Lodge, a pioneer psychic investigator, said it for many of us about animals and ghosts: "We human beings live in a world teeming with sounds we cannot hear, colors and light we cannot see, odors we cannot smell and presences we cannot feel. It is a world in which animals repeatedly demonstrate that they possess what to us is an unexplainable sixth sense."

Jim the Wonder Dog

An all-time demonstration of this sixth sense is one of Missouri's great mysteries, Jim the Wonder Dog. Joel M. Vance, writing about him for *The Missouri Conservationist* in 1990, said "...the dog's abilities were inexplicable and somewhat frightening." Jim has inspired a book and hundreds of magazine articles, which still continue to appear.

Jim was not a ghost, but many people said their hair rose at seeing him correctly "answer" complex questions and make predictions that came true. A frequent reaction to Jim was "That dog is spooky!" Some people who feel that spirits can attach themselves to the living and function through them might agree that Jim was a vehicle for some St. Francis-like entity who hoped to change humankind's disregard for the value of animals.

Jim was born on March 10, 1925, in the state of Louisiana, a descendent from Llewellyn setters with top field performance rankings. His breeder, a man named Taylor, sent him to Sam Van Arsdale, then living in West Plains, Missouri, as a sort of gag gift. Even as a puppy, Jim didn't seem quite right for his breed, being less active than his littermates, with oversized front feet and eyes so expressive and human-like that they made people uncomfortable.

Sam did not take to Jim at first. He was an avid quail hunter who traveled all over the United States and into Canada for his sport. So before investing in a trainer Sam gave Jim to a little niece to play with to see how his temperament was. The games the two youngsters devised were remarkable and Jim went on to be trained as a hunting dog. In his first outing, however, in a hot, dry field, he did not show much promise—just moving from shady spot to shady spot—not searching for birds as the others did. When Sam heard this, he said he would give Jim away, but the trainer said there was a lot to him and he should have another chance. On his next outing, the mystery was solved: birds were present there and Jim worked like an experienced dog. The trainer knew that there had been no birds in the first field, but the puppies didn't know that. Apparently Jim did.

What beck-ning ghost

along the moonlight shade

Invites my steps?

Alexander Pope,
"Elegy to the Memory of an Unfortunate Lady"

For a couple of years, Jim was just an outstanding hunting dog, his eyes continuing to bring comment from everyone who came around him. Sam's wife often remarked that he seemed to understand everything she said to him and one day when they were on a picnic, she asked him if he could show her a certain kind of tree. He went and put his foot on it, looking back at her as if relieved that he finally had an opportunity to show what he could do. When the couple asked Jim to identify other types of trees he went from one to another, correctly identifying each one.

After these events, Jim gradually became a celebrity. At first his owner just demonstrated to people how the dog could pick out a man wearing a vest or a woman in a blue dress. Then it got to be such questions as who had two chows at home and who had never stayed at a hotel before. It was even discovered that Jim could locate cars by color or by being shown a license plate number—even if the car was in the next block.

Sam began putting questions in more complex form. "Jim," he'd say, "if we want to keep our money safe from Al Capone, *where do we put it?*" (Rather than "show us the safe.") Jim even demonstrated that he could respond correctly to questions from other people, in other languages, and most importantly—when Sam was not present. This last point is vital, since "wonder" animals of the past have usually been found to depend on subtle body language from their owners. Even when Sam was present with Jim, he often had his back turned, or held a cigar in his mouth and both hands in his pockets, making it impossible to help his dog "cheat."

Many people consider Jim's predictions as conclusively supernatural. Using pictures or written words, he correctly foretold the outcomes of sporting events and elections—even the sex of unborn children. Jim was examined by expert and skeptical trainers and by many veterinarians, who admitted they could see no explanation for his acts and that perhaps he possessed some special kind of intelligence humankind does not yet understand.

Sam turned down many rich offers to buy Jim, take him on tour, or to participate in publicity stunts such as having him photographed with Franklin Roosevelt, whose election he'd predicted. But instead, the Van Arsdales preferred to give their aging dog a quiet life, as just a cherished pet and friend. When he died of a heart attack, on March 18, 1937, they had a coffin built to fit him and planned to bury him in the family plot in Marshall. This was denied, despite the huge amount of flowers that arrived, testifying to public opinion about Jim. The cemetery board suggested burying him right outside the entrance where those who wanted to see his grave could find it easily. Ironically, the cemetery has grown so much that Jim is now inside it, with his modest grave marker. For decades, people have come from all over the country to see his grave.

The nearest simile I can find

to express the difficulty of sending a message—

I appear to be standing behind

a sheet of frosted glass—dictating feebly

to a reluctant and obtuse secretary.

F.W.H. Myers, through a medium five years after his death,
Society of Psychical Research

As this book was being written, arrangements were being made to place a tribute to Jim in downtown Marshall. This monument will be on the lot where Van Arsdale's hotel—Jim's home—stood. A decorative brick wall and flower garden will create a suitable setting for a life-sized bronze statue.

Evelyn Counts, a Marshall woman who has taken a leading role in this effort, says she has been contacted by several people interested in doing something more with Jim's story than has been done up until now—one of which is a California film producer. The useful thing about all this is that each time Jim's story is told, it will remind us—as the best ghost stories do—that we still don't know everything.

Chapter Twelve

Three Great Mysteries

We may or may not believe in ghosts, ESP, UFOs, or anything else beyond our everyday experience, but Missouri has three other documented happenings, in addition to Jim the Wonder Dog, that defy explanation. They are found in books about the otherworldly, both those done shallowly for sensation and those carefully reporting scholarly study.

One event concerns an instance of what is today called "channeling" that has too much substance and complexity to be laughed away. Another is a natural light occurrence our species will someday probably understand, but which is at present just an enjoyably scary novelty. The third phenomenon seems to demonstrate some of the worst the unknown can do.

Patience Worth

One Missouri phenomenon from the early 20th century has been described as, "The most tantalizing case in psychical research...and the greatest of all literary riddles." It was contact, via Ouija board, from an entity who said her name was Patience Worth, that she was born in the 1600s in England and died in the U.S. in an Indian raid. She then proceeded, for more than a decade, to produce millions of words of conversation, maxims, poetry, prose, and drama. People flocked to St. Louis to witness sittings by her channeler, and they eagerly bought her work, in this country and elsewhere, in the form of magazine articles and as books by New York book publisher, Henry Holt.

O, that it were possible, we might

But hold some two day's conference

with the dead!

Duchess of Malfi, speech of character in a play

The channeling began in July of 1913, when two St. Louis friends, Pearl Curran and Edith Hutchings, joined the fad of playing "Weedj," a game board painted with letters and numbers. Supposedly these could be used by spirits to spell out answers to questions, if two human operators provided physical means by resting their fingers lightly on a little wooden marker. A few weeks' worth of effort had brought the ladies nothing but some sentence fragments—garbled material that seemed to be vaguely religious in content. Then, suddenly one night, the marker began moving decisively and clearly spelled out "Many moons ago I lived. Again I come. My name Patience Worth."

Mrs. Curran's mother copied down the string of letters that followed, and when these had been divided into words and sentences, they promised important messages to come. Over the next several weeks, Patience Worth became a strong presence for this group of friends, their friends' friends, and neighbors. A popular newspaper writer, Caspar Yost, heard of it and the *Globe-Democrat* carried a series of his articles which incorporated what the mysterious entity said about death and the hereafter. Yost also published samples of Patience Worth's poems.

Another St. Louis literary personage, William Marion Reedy, was also intrigued by Patience Worth. He was the editor of a widely respected magazine in which he'd "discovered" a number of writers. Though he accepted nothing Curran relayed about Patience's origin, he said what they were producing was "near genius" and needed to be preserved. His endorsement, with growing public interest in the Patience phenomenon, influenced New York publisher Henry Holt to publish a book Yost wrote about her, and then two subsequent novels that came through Curran.

Long before this, Patience Worth had begun manifesting without the need for Edith Hutchings' help, or even use of the the board. Curran found she could utter letters and then words as fast as she could speak, and she said the fiction was accompanied in her brain by colorful scenes. She visited New York and Chicago and other cities to accommodate crowds interested in Patience. Audience members included Amy Lowell, Hamlin Garland, Fannie Hurst, Upton Sinclair, Edgar Lee Masters and other celebrity writers of the time. Many famous entertainers, such as Ethel Barrymore and Mr. and Mrs. Douglas Fairbanks also came to her gatherings.

The Currans and some supporters even started a magazine devoted to Patience Worth's work, but it lasted for only a few months because interest in the riddle inevitably faded. Then in 1922, John Curran died, leaving his wife with a young daughter and another child on the way.

After a short period of traveling about and doing readings in clubs and private homes, Pearl Curran moved to California, where one dedicated

We experience in different modes.
We perceive external realities,
we dream, imagine, have semi-conscious reveries.
Some people have visions, hallucinations,
experience faces transfigured, see auras and so on.

R.D. Laing, "Transcendental Experience"

Patience supporter offered her some help. She tried to make more money by writing, but she was met with little success—her work being compared unfavorably to what had come through her earlier. Pearl Curran died in California in late 1937, her last reading on Thanksgiving day having been a moving prayer of gratitude from Patience, for having had the opportunity to reveal helpful truths. Curran told her friends Patience had warned her of imminent death, though they were still surprised by her departure, for her health had not seemed that delicate.

Though to the world Patience Worth ended with Pearl Curran, in reality we're told, she continued channeling through one of Mrs. Curran's daughters. This individual apparently did it reluctantly, and only with a small group of friends. One Missourian, Dr. Irene Hickman of Kirksville, published poetry dictated by Patience Worth in this era. Hickman, a long-term devotee, collected and studied Curran's channeling materials for years.

Patience Worth drew many to share a conviction stated by Walter Franklin Prince, an investigator whose *The Case of Patience Worth* is the most complete study ever done on the subject. In 1927 he said, "Either our concept of what we call the subconscious must be radically altered...or else some cause operating through, but not originating in, the subconscious of Mrs. Curran must be acknowledged. In the former case we normalize what would have seemed 'supernormal'...in the second case we admit the supernormal."

At least once a generation comes a revival of interest in Patience Worth. The half dozen books and other writings about her are studied anew, as are Pearl Curran's own apparent writings. Findings of past investigators are pondered—and still no one, no matter how skeptical, has presented a theory or evidence, as to how Patience Worth could have been a hoax.

Reasons include a lack of motive and the impossibility of figuring out how the Currans could have done it. The couple was well-off when Patience Worth first manifested, and was not at all secure at the ends of their lives. The fact that Pearl Curran was hard put to support herself proved that they had not profited from Patience Worth. Indeed, the husband once said in an interview that they had lost a great deal of money on the magazine devoted to Patience Worth and that he'd spent at least $4,000 on the comfort of people who came to their house for readings. They had never charged for these. Additional expenses were incurred when the Currans hired stenographers and typists to help handle Patience's materials.

It is also doubtful that the Currans were doing all of this for attention, since most of the attention they received was negative. Pearl Curran once told an interviewer that she was looked at with distrust by some of her friends and with awe by others—in both cases losing relationships. In addition to straining close ties, she was often ridiculed in print and on radio,

Not a disembodied spirit
can the weapons of tyrants let loose,
But it stalks invisibly over the earth,
whispering, counseling, cautioning.

Walt Whitman, "Leaves of Grass"

and the schedule of readings she kept, often many nights in a row, was fatiguing and stressful.

While none of the three literary figures in Curran's life—Yost, Reedy and Holt—ever conceded Patience was exactly what Curran said she was, they gave the St. Louis resident vital support. Yost pointed out that any writer who could produce such work would not be likely to present it as another person's and in obscure language that made public enjoyment difficult. Reedy remarked that with writing so time-consuming at best, nobody would opt to compose in secret and memorize everything and then sit and transmit it to the relatively few people who could and would come to listen.

Investigators could find nothing in Pearl Curran's background to suggest that she, alone, was capable of doing such writing. As a schoolgirl she had little interest in anything but music and she was allowed to end her education at the age of 13. She had never cared about history or England and no later change in attitude could be found. Religion had only a small place in Curran's childhood and none in her adult life. No interest in serious literature or writing could be uncovered. What she did read was light fiction—and not much of that. Curran's home did not even contain books pertaining to anything Patience talked about and there was no evidence that the Currans checked any such materials out of libraries.

Curran's home didn't include any area hinting that research or writing was going on. Mrs. Curran did not spend time in seclusion; she kept her usual schedule of socializing, shopping and managing a house that was, while not luxurious, more than just comfortable. She was considered by her friends to be a pleasant, uncomplicated, and unpretentious person. Her stepdaughter said Pearl Curran was not capable of conceiving a hoax or carrying it off.

Then there was the question of how anyone could memorize and deliver, without errors and at conversational pace, the amount of material Pearl Curran relayed in sittings often lasting two hours. Nobody could do it, even if devoting each day to what would be recited that night. An additional question: how could polished, graceful poetry be produced impromptu when audience members suggested topics Mrs. Curran could have no way of anticipating? This was a frequent feature of her sittings.

Also baffling was the general quality and content of her work, declared by experts of the time to be superb. Today's critics would be much less impressed, because it is wordy and flowery, but that was the admired mode until the last few decades. Few of today's readers would stay with most of the prose, laboriously reproducing speech patterns and difficult vocabulary of another time and place. Those who knew, though, said that factually everything was exactly right for the 1600s in the area where Patience Worth

I yanked on his blanket,

but my poor transparent fingers

poked right through it.

I darted over to where his lifejacket

hung on the peg, but my hands

scooped through it like a fork into whipped cream.

I couldn't have lifted a matchstick,

let alone a lifejacket,

for I was ghost, haunting the past.

Richard Peck, "Ghosts I Have Been"

said she grew up and for the Eastern and Bible Land settings of her fiction and drama. One religious expert said Patience Worth's attitudes were typical of the liberal Quakers of her era. Her messages are explored in more detail in Appendix A.

Perhaps in the near future, someone will figure Patience Worth out. Maybe as more science fiction comes true, all the great untapped brains of the past will be channeled. For the present, Missouri holds its position in annals of the supranormal for having what Dr. Prince called "the most amazing case of its kind in history."

The Spook Light

Technically, this phenomenon of moving, varicolored lights is not Missouri's, for its main activity is just across the state line on Oklahoma soil, but Missouri roads have given innumerable people an unaccountable sight. These roads can be picked up near Hornet, a hamlet south of Joplin. And although the spook light is not what's usually thought of as a ghost, it inspires in viewers the same sort of disbelief and uneasiness as ghost sightings do. Like the whole subject of ghosts, it is just one of those things we do not, at this time, understand.

Here are a few of the many Spook Light (also called Indian Light or Hornet Light) descriptions:

❖ A ball of orangey yellow fire that may or may not radiate heat as it goes by.
❖ A blue-silver ball or a ball made up of many balls of many colors.
❖ Two greenish, bluish balls that spin against each other.
❖ A purple bubble, that is diamond- or oval-shaped at times.
❖ Light concentrating itself into the size of a golf ball, too blindingly bright to look at.

Most commonly, the light swings or bobs back and forth across the road, varying in size from about that of a basketball to that of a bushel basket, its altitude varying from ground level to treetop. However, when under intense observation, the light has been reported to come speeding down the road and just before impact with a car or person, lift up, fly over and come down behind them and continue on. It's said to usually retreat from whatever advances toward it. If shot at, it may burst into a fireworks-like blizzard of tiny lights or bubbles and then reassemble, but it has also been reported to do this without being shot at.

A queer sensation of fear passed over him,
a faintness and shiver down the back.
It went however, and he was debating
whether to call aloud to his invisible visitor,
or slam the door and return to his books,
when the cause of his disturbance
turned the corner slowly
and came into view.

Algernon Blackwood, "Best Ghost Stories"

Some people have declared that the light followed their car as they left the scene. One resident said the spook light spent an evening on his porch and at times seemed to be looking in the front window. In another story, the spook light appeared at the barn door one night when a family was milking their cows and blocked their exit for a long, nerve-wracking time. The spook has been called "very consistent, performing almost every night in all weather at all times of year." It's even been reported in daylight.

Of course many explanatory stories have been created since 1886—the date usually given for the light's first appearance. Since Choctaws originally dwelled upon the land where the lights appear, people created many legends about what the lights were. Some believe they were the spirits of young lovers kept apart by cruel elders, or of a lost chieftain trying to find his way home. Because the light's area includes some mining, there were stories on that theme too. In one story, a miner looks for his children stolen by Indians or for something he has lost along the path. There's even a Civil War story, about a deserter executed by cannon fire. The most thoughtful story is that the light somehow commemorates sufferings of exiled Cherokees on the infamous Trail of Tears, struggling through the general area in the winter of 1838-39, enroute from their homes in the South to Indian Territory in what became Oklahoma.

Many groups have even studied the spook light using scientific methods. They have accomplished little more than to disprove some of the easiest theories—that the light is swamp gas, St. Elmo's fire, will-o-the-wisp or light refracted from car headlights. Swamp gas requires the presence of more water than exists in the Hornet area and it gives off a distinctive sulphury odor. St. Elmo's fire is always attached to something that is electrically charged and does not move about freely on its own. Will-o'-the-Wisp is seen over extended masses of decaying organic matter, not over dry roads or open fields. The idea that car lights are refracting from highways out of sight of the viewing road called Devil's Promenade might be accepted except that the Spook Light was reported long before cars or highways ever existed.

Experiences of Missourians with less ambitious lights than the one near Hornet are also worth a little analysis. Judy Grundler of Columbia tells of lights that three generations of her relatives saw on their farm. These mini-spooks were small and bluish-white, usually seen across a certain field, in pretty much the same spot and only occasionally approaching closer, observed only one time up on the lawn of the house. She says that they were consistent in showing up, and in disappearing as cars went by.

Among the Bittersweet collection was a brief story of two men driving home in a wagon after a hard day's work at logging. Unaccountably their tired horses became agitated enough that the men leaped out, each going to

*As I groped my way over to the mantelpiece
to find the matches I realized all at once
that there was a person standing beside me
in the darkness. I could, of course, see nothing,
but my fingers, feeling along the ledge,
came into forcible contact with something
that was at once withdrawn.
It was cold and moist.*

Algernon Blackwood, "Best Ghost Stories"

a horse's head to quiet it. From that position they could see, from some distance behind them, a large, brilliant light in the road. As they watched, it sped forward and quickly overtook them. They had time only to lower their heads against the horses' necks before it swept over them and on down the road ahead and out of sight. This happened somewhere in the Ozarks, but was presented as a one-time oddity, not an instance of the spook light.

Another interviewee who preferred not to be identified repeated a family story from her mother's time, when the family lived on a farm near Braggadocio, far down in the Missouri's bootheel. Almost every evening, a single ball of orange fire would roll down a particular tree trunk, across the ground and under the porch. It never did any harm, but it frightened the children and made neighbors unwilling to visit after dark. Far-fetched as that may sound, it could lead us to something, for another part of the story is that a friend who was a woodsman told them he'd often seen this phenomenon. He said it happened in only one kind of tree and that was the kind they had by their porch.

Eugene Brunk, assistant state forester for 13 years with the Missouri Department of Conservation, says that trees which are rotting inside can produce quite a lot of methane gas. In taking core samples, he has heard the gas escaping from pierced trees and has seen instances when there was enough escaping that it could be lit and would burn for up to ten minutes. Methane gas may escape less dramatically through cracks in bark, and it can reflect light shining on it, Brunk says. Is it possible then, that with temperature changes, a tree cracked down its length could release gas that would reflect the light of lamps in a house as it followed a crack down exposed roots that went under a porch?

"Maybe..." Brunk said. This would be a long shot, and is far removed from antics of the Hornet Light, but may indicate a principle that will some-day be found to apply.

One theory about spook lights is that they could be caused by the ground beneath them. For instance, the area in Texas where the incredibly profitable Spindletop Oil Well was developed had for decades been noted for weird lights that danced over it. Still another possibility might be the underground movements associated with earthquakes. In the summer before Missouri's great quakes of 1811-12, strange lights and odors were widely reported in the area of New Madrid where the quakes occurred. Missouri's famous Spook Light appears in a fault area.

To see the Spook Light, instructions from Joplin City Hall are: "take I-44 west from Joplin to 43 Highway. Drive south on 43 approximately six miles to BB Highway. Turn right and drive approximately three miles to the road's end. Turn right and drive another mile to the second dirt road on

*Ghosts! There are nigh a thousand million
walking the earth openly at noontide.
O Heaven, it is mysterious, it is awful
to consider that we not only carry each a future
ghost within, but are, in very deed, ghosts!*

Thomas Carlyle

the left. You will see a little building on the right and are now headed west on "Spook Light Road." Park anywhere along the side of the road and wait. Approximately 1.5 miles down the road is the best and the darkest."

An Unpleasant Exclusive

Another Missouri exclusive in the annals of the supernatural inspired a book and a movie, both named *The Exorcist*, which most people have seen or heard about. The main differences between fact and fiction are that the victim of the apparent possession was a boy—not a girl—and that no one died as a result of the combat with demons. The real-life episode lasted for about three months and was resolved. The victim, now in his 60s, was freed and continues to live a normal life. Here's what happened, according to *Possessed: The True Story of an Exorcism*, by Thomas B. Allen.

In 1949, the life of a Maryland family named Mannheim (changed for the purposes of the report) living in a suburb of Washington, D.C., was disrupted when their son became the focus of strange happenings. Robbie (again, not the true name) was almost fourteen and had been spending a lot of time playing with a Ouiji board. He'd been introduced to this by an aunt who had recently died. Robbie's parents didn't monitor his use of the game. They later said that they had no idea what he was asking the board or whether he thought it was giving him contact with his aunt.

The first happenings were puzzling and mildly annoying sounds. Water dripped where there were no leaky faucets, and some animal seemed to be clawing wood, though no source could be found. The next eerie occurrence was what sounded like someone marching back and forth in squeaky shoes beside Robbie's bed. Several family members heard this. The sounds soon became more disturbing, as the clawing seemed to come from within Robbie's mattress. Then a large, heavy chair lifted itself from the floor, tipped sideways and dumped Robbie out. His father and uncles were unable to tip the same chair when exerting all their weight and strength to do so. At a friend's house, a rocker Robbie sat in began spinning wildly. At school his desk-chair moved out into the aisle and glided around as if on runners.

Understandably, Robbie became upset. He was allowed to drop out of school, but this didn't help. He began to wake up at night screaming, and his family sometimes heard him muttering in his sleep in strange voices, often spouting obscenities. Sometimes the voices threatened harm to family members. Scratches began to appear on Robbie's body, sometimes suggesting a taloned paw, sometimes spelling out N-O.

The Mannheims could not dismiss this as the hoax of a mentally ill child. They had seen such things as a dresser moving across the bedroom to

Silky ghosts are female spirits
who dress in elaborate silk attire
to tend to domestic chores
in houses where lazy servants live.

Anonymous

block Robbie's bedroom door, its drawers zipping in and out as if someone were searching through them frantically. So they sought help from doctors, psychologists and ministers, but no one knew what to do. Their own Lutheran minister prayed with Robbie and the family. Their friends and church members organized a special prayer circle. When all of this seemed fruitless, the minister suggested calling on a Catholic priest, since that denomination does not dismiss the idea of devils as most others do.

The priest who agreed to help had Robbie taken to a Catholic hospital where he would be surrounded by dedicated Christians and by symbols of religion. He had Robbie put in restraints to control his growing violence which included spitting on people and kicking at all who approached him. In spite of this, Allen writes, Robbie somehow got a piece of bedspring loose and raked it with such force down the whole length of the priest's arm that the wound took more than a hundred stitches to close.

In early March, about a month after the initial problems began, the family took Robbie to St. Louis where they had relatives and where there was a concentration of Jesuit priests. St. Louis University was founded by the Catholic Society of Jesus order and is still operated by Jesuits. A team of three spent many nights with Robbie. They prayed around his bed and used ancient rituals that command demons to depart.

Despite these steps, all symptoms grew worse. Robbie flailed about as if doing strenuous exercises for longer than seemed humanly possible. He laughed wildly. He destroyed the priests' prayer books and attacked anyone who came close enough, breaking one priest's nose, causing another's to bleed. Robbie threw his food around the room and sang for hours—often obscene songs from long-gone eras of history.

At one point, however, one of the boy's strange, deep voices said Robbie would not be free until he, himself, called on Jesus for help. This seemed to be the turning point. The priests turned their efforts to using Robbie's few rational moments to make baptism possible. The actual ceremony took place only after a four-hour physical struggle with Robbie protesting and cursing throughout. Amidst it all, however, the priests heard Robbie say, as if to himself, "I do renounce Satan and all his work."

The problems didn't end immediately, but at 10:45 the next morning a clear, rich voice said through Robbie, "I am Saint Michael and I command you, Satan, and the other evil spirits to leave this body. . .Now! Now! Now!" After a few more minutes of struggle, Robbie grew quiet and announced in his own voice, "He's gone." A great explosive sound ripped through the hospital, heard by all who were there. A little later, Robbie took communion, ate and had a deep sleep. He awoke asking where he was and seemed to have little memory of the ordeal he and many others had been through.

Be careful not to conjure up
more phantoms than you can put down.

Old Proverb

Though the priests working with Robbie had been told by their superiors not to make any record of the experience, some of them did. Earlier, his parents and others had written down what was happening. Allen was grateful for this, saying it made Robbie's the best-documented case of exorcism in our time. And it happened in Missouri.

Regardless of anyone's feeling about the supernatural, the fact remains that Missouri has several of the most studied and documented mysteries in history: the case of Patience Worth, the Hornet Spook Light, Jim the Wonder Dog and the "Robbie Mannheim" Exorcism. As study continues, these may eventually make our state famous as the place where major questions were answered.

Chapter Thirteen

When a Body Meets a Nonbody

Anyone who collects ghost stories soon finds that most of them fall into categories. Some are fabrications, spun out by fun-loving story-tellers like my cousin Ed. Other ghostly doings are pranks like the one at Christian College. And some are drama created and enacted for a serious purpose—like the Ozark man on his deathbed, who had a young descendant brought to him and said, "It's time for me to tell you how to do the *h'ant* that keeps people away from our still." Some ghostly encounters told in complete sincerity are illusion—we all know that stress, some drugs and sleep deprivation can cause hallucinations of sight, sound or smell. Encounters of this variety, accepted as supernatural, are honest mistakes or uncertainty.

A perfect example came as this book was almost done, from a young relative who adamantly disbelieves in ghosts, ESP, UFOs and whatever else that can even remotely be termed occult or supernatural. She surprised me with this story about a ride she took on her Arab mare, accompanied by a very large white dog.

"There were only a few more nights left to see the Hale-Bopp comet, so I got on Crissy bareback and we went down the road a half mile or so to that open field that gives a good view of the sky. Emmarose was the only dog

Many people recounting ghostly visits
describe a drop in the surrounding temperature
just before the ghost appears,
or a thickening of the atmosphere
—as if, according to one observer,
"the room seemed to get very full of people."

Anonymous, "Phantom Encounters"

who came along. When we passed where the pointers live, I was watching for them, though Crissy is never alarmed by dogs and Emmarose is getting accustomed to these particular ones. They didn't come out, which is unusual.

"Just past there, at that brushy curve, I saw a dog standing looking across the road. In the poor light, I didn't recognize it. It looked something like a chow, only taller. I wondered if it might be a coyote. Then it started across the road and I could see that it was crippled. All this time Crissy did not turn her head toward it or move her ears. Emmarose didn't look either, and the dog never looked at us. It was really creepy, as if no dog were actually there or we were not there for it to see. It had to have heard us coming on the gravel. It made a sort of circle out in the field, and then moved into the trees. I would never have thought animals could be so close together and none of them acknowledge the others, especially when one of them was doing something unusual."

We talked about the fact that a neighbor, considerably farther away on an intersecting road, used to have a pair of chows, but we'd not seen them for so long we doubted if they were still there. We wondered if someone had dumped out an injured dog, or a stray had been hit by a car. We agreed to watch for the chows or for any new dog in the area and for a limping coyote. Within a week we passed the crossroads and saw the two chows with a taller companion who looked like a chow mix and appeared to have a missing hind foot. So much for what could have been a good story—the limping ghost of Hartley Road! And so much for the commonly accepted idea that if animals don't react to other animals, some of them must be present in spirit only.

What explains this incident? Maybe the air was moving across all souls at a right angle, not dropping any clues. Maybe the lame dog is deaf and sight-impaired. Maybe they all became well acquainted in their nighttime lives which we humans know nothing about, so that meeting on the road was a non-event to them.

As we explore other ghostly occurrences, we find still another category of story—those involving natural, but far-fetched explanations. In 1895 the *Missouri Patriot* reprinted a Des Moines newspaper story telling of the end of a "peg-legged ghost" that had haunted one of its hotels for a decade. Many people had heard, through many nights, the sound of a normal and a strange footstep in sequence down one particular hall. Rooms there were hard to rent, so the proprietor finally decided to replace the floor of the hallway. When it was taken up, he found a remarkable explanation for the peg-legged walking. One joist had been grooved out along its whole length to accommodate a line for gaslights, but had not been used that way, for some reason. Rats, however, had found it a most convenient conduit for

This is the dumb and dreary hour,

When injur'd ghosts complain;

When yawning graves give up their dead

to haunt the faithless swain.

David Mallet, "William & Margaret"

travel, so much so that their moving bodies actually rounded off sharp edges of the groove. They were heavy enough that their movement caused the imperfectly seated joist to raise up and down against other boards, and this created sounds that frightened people for years and cost the hotel owner quite a lot of money.

Categories of Ghosts

Just as stories have categories, so do ghosts. Different types of spirits do different things. Banshees vocalize in an unearthly manner and poltergeists make noises, throw things around and sometimes get credit for starting fires. Any dictionary or thesaurus gives an incredible number of synonyms for the word ghost: apparition, phantom, wraith, revenant and doppelganger, to name just a few. An apparition is something we can see, and perhaps phantoms and wraiths are too. Revenant just means "returning" or "one who comes back." Some boats are given this name for obvious reasons. Doppelgangers, as we saw with Mark Twain, are the doubles of living people.

Psychic investigators also speak of "thought forms," which were used to explain an event in Maries County. A couple reported the regular presence in their home of a pleasant looking elderly woman. She was no threat to anyone and caused no disturbance; they would just see her at the kitchen counter, in the rocking chair, and at the curtains. Finally they described her to enough people that someone said "she sounds just like a woman who used to live in your house; she's still alive, in a nursing home near here." The couple went to visit her, and indeed it was; she told them how she had loved the house and how often she thought about her happy life there with her husband of decades. They said nothing about seeing her and resigned themselves to sharing the house with her memory self.

Complicating the matter of ghosts is the fact that two of the synonyms commonly given are spirit and soul. Even in the Bible, the three words are often used interchangeably, and we hardly notice: Holy Ghost; "...he gave up the ghost"; "...the spirit returns to God who gave it"; "tonight thy soul will be required of thee." It's interesting that airlines and ships speak of their passenger lists in terms of souls aboard and different groups attribute different qualities to some of these terms. For instance, Jehovah's Witnesses feel that our bodies and souls are inseparable, that each of us is a soul, not a body serving as vehicle for a spirit. They feel that all living things are souls, not just human beings.

The iron tongue of midnight

hath told twelve;

Lovers, to bed,

'tis almost fairy time.

Shakespeare, "A Midsummer Night's Dream"

Why Does It Matter?

We who collect ghost stories soon become aware of just how intensely interested other people are. We find that some of the most used—and most stolen—library books are those featuring ghosts. The popularity of mystery novels turning on the supernatural is undying. As this was written a whole new category of romance novels was developing, those in which living people are in love with ghosts. It's a big surprise to see in books of quotations how many prominent and respected people over the centuries have speculated about ghosts. Why does our species care so much? Some of these quotations explain it clearly. Robert Blair, a British poet of the 1700s, wrote in a poem called "The Grave":

> *Tell us, ye dead! Will none of you in pity*
> *To those you left behind disclose the secret?*
> *Oh! That some courteous ghost would blab it out!*
> *What 'tis you are, and we must shortly be.*

Another British writer, J. B. Priestley, commented on the fact that so little of what comes from the supposed hereafter in seances and various psychic readings has any real importance for our lives. He asked why those in spirit, who should be in a position to give us invaluable information, rarely choose to do so. He suspected that we can hope for nothing from them that is beyond the medium's knowledge. Priestly insisted that if spirits have any power to do anything or communicate anything, our departed loved ones would constantly use their ability to protect and guide us.

This brings us back to that great Missouri exclusive, Patience Worth. While there have been a few instances of channeling that offered elaborate descriptions of the hereafter and suggestions for how we should be living, what Pearl Curran gave us, as from Patience Worth, seems the most concise, logical and usable. It appears in Appendix A.

But What If We Meet One?

This is the bottom line with many fans of ghost stories: regardless of what ghosts are or what their intentions are or what they know, how do we protect ourselves against them? Fascinating as they are, most of us would join Alfred, Lord Tennyson, in questioning whether we really want our departed loved ones hovering around all the time, watching us and tuning in on our thoughts.

For advice on dealing with ghosts, Missourians are lucky. We have three widely recognized expert psychical investigators. They are Bevy Jaegers

The search for proof
of the existence of ghosts
has consumed the time and energy
of any number of scientists,
psychical investigators,
and ghost hunters
over the years.
Most have toiled quietly in obscurity.

Anonymous, "Phantom Encounters"

of St. Louis, Maurice Schwalm of Kansas City and Dr. Irene Hickman of Kirksville. Their outlooks vary but are mainly reassuring. Jaegers and Schwalm see most discarnate (bodiless) entities as basically harmless and not especially interested in us; Dr. Hickman takes the demonic side of the supernatural more seriously but tells us how to avoid it. More data about each of these people appears in Appendix B.

Jaegers has studied psychic phenomena for decades, has written extensively about them and conducted seminars and classes. Her view is that most so-called ghosts have agendas of their own and are only occasionally interested in us. "They have no power over us except the power to frighten, and I don't believe many of them try to do that." She points out that most injury reported from ghostly encounters comes from someone falling or otherwise getting hurt in a panicked retreat and, less often, from heart symptoms. Taking a calm view of ghosts can prevent that and her attitude helps us.

Jaegers says that if the apparition appears aware of you, or perhaps makes an entreating gesture, it's best to say something like "I'm sorry I can't help you, but if you put out your hand and look for the light, you will find a better place than this."

She says a great many manifestations are from spirits of people who died under circumstances that left them confused about whether they are dead or alive. Some are unusually fearful of going to another level of existence. Some are deeply attached to people or places or possessions. When she worked with a team of investigators, their procedure in places reputed to be haunted was just to give the message of looking for the light and going to the better things available there. In most cases that seemed to work. Jaegers adds that praying can give courage in such situations. She and those in her group frequently prayed, alone or together.

Jaegers repeats that dangers from evil spirits are minimal, saying, "It's more a matter of being *obsessed* than *possessed*." She reminds us it's easy for someone in a vulnerable emotional state, from bereavement or another crisis, to damage physical and mental health by dwelling on the idea of communicating with the departed. As many charlatans operate in the field of parapsychology as anywhere else, she says. They often offer help that is impossible to produce and prey on those who believe them. People tend to accept the expertise of these people much more easily than they would accept it in another field. She says that if anyone wants help from a psychic or parapsychologist, they should go at it in the same way they'd look for any professional help, drawing on the experience and references of people who have some way of knowing who can be trusted. Local law enforcers often know who, in the area, works in a businesslike way and whose results can be rated for accuracy. Doctors may know this, too, especially psychologists.

Spirits are supernatural beings

with appearances ranging

from elves to demons,

and they may even represent places,

such as the spirits of lakes or mountains.

Anonymous

Bevy Jaegers warns against looking for answers from Ouija boards, seances and such. Resuming and retaining the best of one's normal life is usually a far more effective cure for problems.

Schwalm says "...if you meet a ghost, you should feel honored, for not very many people have this experience." He warns though, that chances are you'll never know it, because most apparitions look perfectly real. He agrees with Jaegers that few ghosts have any bad intent toward us. Sometimes they just want to be noticed and, like a tiresome child, can be deflected by being ignored. "If you feel a touch, or see or hear or smell something, just go ahead with what you're doing," he says.

Schwalm has found that wearing or holding a cross seems to have a protective effect for many people, and he suggests that any kind of sacramental object, even from a faith not your own, can give this benefit. He too, suggests prayer, remarking that Silent Unity, a program of perpetual prayer offered by Unity Centers in many cities, is a good refuge in these cases. He often asks for remembrance from the Kansas City group when he undertakes an investigation he feels is potentially dangerous. Another self-protecting move he suggests is to visualize oneself surrounded by white light.

⅋ For those tempted to experiment with the occult, Schwalm's main warning is to realize that something troublesome may come home with you from a seance. He says that in a place reputed to be haunted one should not go into deep meditation. Do nothing more than close the eyes briefly to see what impressions may come. He says people with tendencies to be obsessive should completely avoid deliberate involvement with the supernatural.

At the same time, Schwalm has a cheering thought that would not occur to all of us. "Remember that you at times have around you spirits with a supporting or protective interest. These may be relatives or just someone attracted to you from the astral plane because they want to participate in something positive you're doing."

Like a guardian angel?

"If you want to think of it that way," he says, and adds that there's nothing wrong with invoking protection and help from such beings. One last remark: "Their responses aren't likely to be dramatic messages, just feelings or ideas that seem to be your own."

Dr. Hickman, while agreeing in many ways with the others, feels that much of the world's suffering stems from the attachment to humans of confused, frightened or emotionally disturbed entities. These may be the spirits of people who attach to humans through whom they can continue to experience the things they enjoyed in life. For instance, someone who died

Shojos, or sea ghosts, have vibrant red hair
and an addiction to merriment.
They are harmless spirits who dance
on the waves of every ocean.

Anonymous

from smoking, may attach to a smoker, increasing that person's inability to stop. Sadists will seek out individuals whose activity they can share and perhaps direct.

In Dr. Hickman's philosophy, we're at our most vulnerable when we indulge in activity we know we should avoid, so a great element of self-protection is shunning places and activities that would be enjoyed by evil beings. But, she says, the best of us are vulnerable when exhausted, ill, under anesthesia, depressed or stressed, so we should try to live as full of health as possible. Particularly, she says, we should avoid drugs and alcohol.

One other admonition from Dr. Hickman: "Be militantly independent! Resolve that nobody and no thing is going to dictate to you what you should do or feel or think." She gives an example of her view of how this may work: "In a period when I was using a Ouija board, an entity kept announcing itself as Saul of Tarsus. I was sure it was an impostor, so I just admonished it and put the board away," she said. "Too many people who try these things believe that some celebrity from the past is seeking them out. This is intended to flatter us into accepting all they will then try to tell us to do. If anything like that happens to you, tell them forcefully that you don't buy it and don't want to hear from them again."

Appendix A
What Patience Worth Said

The apparent entity, Patience Worth, was quoted at great length for her clever conversation, her jokes, and for her testiness with people who asked trick questions or otherwise treated her lightly. But predominantly, especially at first, she seemed to want to talk about religion, and her audiences asked many questions about life after death and the nature of God.

Of the next world, Patience Worth said, "Believe me, good souls, life is there as here." Later she said one difference is that there are "days and days and days in what thou wouldst say was hours." She indicated that we still have work to do in spirit form, since one short earthly life does not allow for full development. She admonished that peace and salvation came only from "work and work and work alone." But Patience Worth dismissed the idea of reincarnation, saying "Once uttered, man is forever. Once we cast the flesh, the spirit is free, untrammeled forever."

Her picture of God: "He is our father and his name is Love." She went on reassuringly that, like the best human father, God sympathizes with his children's pain and sorrow, consoling those who allow him to. She said God does not condemn, and that he wants to be loved, not feared. Patience Worth said God never forsakes us, here or in the next world, that when we pray he listens not to our words, but to our spirits. She said his love extends to the tiniest of his creatures, "...e'en the midge whose wing-whirr be all its voice." Finally, of God Patience Worth said, "Nae walls can hold him. Thy heart is afull of him, Brother."

She was encouraging about death, too, calling it "Our Mother," describing it as "...a yawn, a blink and the wakin'." She said that on any terms death "is small price to pay" for the pleasures of life here and the life to come. When asked if we will be reunited on the other side with those we loved here, she replied, "Farewells are something of Earth that must be unlearned."

What Patience Worth said in her poetry was sometimes humorous, always appreciative of nature, very often focused on social comment far ahead of her time or of Pearl Curran's. For instance, in an era when the inevitability and gloriousness of war was unquestioned, she presented several stanzas graphically showing its horrors. Each stanza ended, "Father, is this thy will?" She compared the potential of individual women with the restrictions forced on all women and pointed out the injustice of inescapable childbearing in a poem with this ending:

> For womankind goeth through the valley of death
> In darkness, with no taper for to lighten,
> Leading man to the brink of day
> And he, finding the day made perfect
> Through the agony of womankind,
> Struts!

Patience Worth always showed great compassion and appreciation for children, and she proposed a replacement for the standard child's prayer which reminds them each night that they may die in their sleep. She offered these touching lines:

> I, thy child forever, play
> About thy knees, this close of day.
> Into thy arms I soon will creep,
> To learn thy wisdom while I sleep.

Often, when Patience Worth wrote about nature, her voice did not sound as if it came from another century. Two samples:

> I think of the hushing of leaves...
> And of the weaving of the wind, in and about,
> Or the rustle of some field folk, or the shuttle of a wing.
> I think of a deep, dark shadowed place, besplotched of
>   sunlight and shadow;
> And I, Oh my beloved God, in such a place feel at one
>   with thee....
>
> I love waters and dew and frost
> And thorn and young buds, befurred buds.
> I love forsaken nests. I love paths
> Bebriared, leading to deep thickets....

> I love to find a fallen feather or a down-trod bloom,
> ...I love cliffs where the fern clings
> And there is moss, thick, and snails.
> ...these things...are seeds to my soul.

The novels Patience Worth wrote are to most of us, far less interesting than her poetry. The language is too hard, action too slow, conversation and description too drawn out. But, as one of her greatest fans, Dr. Irene Hickman has commented, some judicious editing might regain for them the popularity they had in the 1930s. At that time they were much respected for the details of life they revealed in setting historic scenes. Experts said this information was eerily accurate, but inaccessible to all but dedicated scholars. The total of it, they said, was unbelievable to have been absorbed by one individual.

Patience Worth's most successful novel, probably, was the one called *A Sorry Tale*. It described parallel lives of Jesus and a man born on the same night. The two grew up in the same area, their paths crossing casually occasionally, but they did not really meet until Calvary (the hill where executions took place), where they were crucified together.

Altogether, the writings of Patience Worth now occupy almost 30 books, some still in typescript. Her most popular ones and those written about her now are out of print and hard to find, except for the one Dr. Hickman produced. For anyone who was intrigued by this remarkable phenomenon, the search would be worth it.

Rather than being studied further, Patience Worth, whatever she was, might prefer that we just remember what she said about serious things, and maybe this one poem:

> My hand, behold it—God's implement!
> With the touch of its flesh I am quickened
> Into a creator;
> Thereby am I a part of Him, given
> An infinitesimal portion of His power...
>
> Behold my hand, the link between earth
> And that splendor which is Eternity;
> For labor is the path unto Redemption.

The book by Walter Franklin Prince, *The Case of Patience Worth*, contains a great many of her poems. Dr. Hickman's, *I Knew Patience Worth*, has mainly poems from the California channelings.

Appendix B
Three Mentors

Bevy Jaegers

B evy Jaegers of St. Louis is probably the best known of Missouri psychic investigators, having figured in a number of interesting police cases in her own area and beyond. One of the most memorable was a murder case in which she led law enforcers to where the victim's body would be found. On another occasion, she predicted a coffee shortage, benefiting a commodities broker so richly that he gave her a house in gratitude. Even more impressive, she remote-viewed the Challenger tragedy, her findings registered in advance through an agency that exists for this purpose. Bevy still spends time working with the Psi team in St. Louis and with law enforcers, but her main pursuit is free-lance writing. Much of this centers on antiques and other subjects far from the supernatural.

One of her most recent major undertakings is a series of books on fingerprints and how they may be used for character analysis as well as identification. The first two published by Berkeley are *Beyond Palmistry: the Art and Science of Modern Hand Analysis* and *Beyond Palmistry II: Your Career is in Your Hands*. The most recent, *The Hands of Children*, was just published. Bevy has, however, done a number of books, articles and educational materials about the psi skills. She has made many media appearances, done many lectures and led many seminars. Bevy has been quoted and interviewed in a number of publications, here and in other countries.

Bevy's approach is always low-key, her view of the supernatural mainly matter of fact. One of her primary interests is how we all can enhance our lives by understanding something of what lies beyond the ordinary.

Dr. Irene Hickman

D r. Irene Hickman of Kirksville, an Iowa native, was featured in a 1975 book, *Psychic Women*, with five others who had discovered unusual abilities they could use in positive ways. From childhood, she told interviewers, she has "just known" certain truths, which led her to study the supernormal from about the age of twelve.

Her profession was osteopathic medicine, and she specialized in psychosomatic cases, with hypnotism as one of her tools. Spontaneous past-life regressions of some patients confirmed her own feeling that reincarnation is a fact and that past lives may affect present ones.

While living in California, Dr. Hickman was part of the group that regularly witnessed the work of one of Pearl Curran's daughters, apparently channeling Patience Worth. As mentioned earlier, Dr. Hickman preserved some of this material, particularly the poetry, and published it in a small book called *I Knew Patience Worth*.

Her experience and study led her to convictions based on the age-old belief that many problems of physical and mental health come from what history calls possession by either earthbound entities or demons. She reminds that the Bible repeatedly shows Jesus "casting out unclean spirits and demons."

In 1994, Dr. Hickman published a book, *Remote Depossession*, which describes how she works in this area. Then, in 1996, with others who share her feelings or are interested in possibilities they raise, she founded the Depossession Institute. This is now a national organization with more than 200 members, including writers, health professionals, and workers in various religious and scientific fields.

Dr. Hickman has written other books and her writings have been anthologized. She also has done lectures and seminars throughout the United States and in eight other countries.

Maurice Schwalm

Maurice Schwalm's name appears in most reports of hauntings from Kansas City and beyond. His role is usually that of psychical investigator, but he often appears on radio or television, and he attests to more than 100 media appearances to share his experiences. He hosted a show on KCMO radio in 1984-85, reporting what he terms "earth mysteries" as well as hauntings. He holds office in his area chapter of Mensa and is listed in the Facts on File *Encyclopedia of Ghosts and Spirits*. Maurice has been published widely in both general and professional magazines. His work appears in several anthologies, one of the more recent being *The Haunted Householder's Handbook*. Maurice is now compiling a book from his experiences and study.

Native to Kansas City, Maurice earned a BA in History at the University of Missouri and added certification in banking and insurance law. In the insurance industry until retirement, he now works full-time as a psychical investigator. His resume says he's visited more than 100 haunted sites. For the person interested in the paranormal, Maurice suggests the book *ESP, Hauntings and Poltergeists: a Parapsychologists' Handbook*, by Lloyd Auerbach.

Bibliography

Books

Archer, Fred. *Exploring the Psychic World.* William Morrow, 1967.

Allen, Thomas B. *Possessed: The True Story of an Exorcism.* Doubleday, 1993.

Animal Ghosts. University Books, 1970.

Auerbach, Lloyd. *ESP, Hauntings and Poltergeists: A Parapsychologists' Handbook.*

Bartlett, John. *Bartlett's Familiar Quotations.* Little, Brown, 1955.

Bayless, Raymond. *Experiences of a Psychical Researcher.* University Books, 1972.

Boswell, Harriett A. *Master Guide to Psychism.* Parker Publishing, 1969.

Buckley, Doris Heather. *Spirit Communication for the Millions.* Dell, 1967.

Caldwell, Dorothy, ed. *Missouri Historical Sites Catalog.* State Historical Society of Missouri–Columbia, 1963.

Cohen, Daniel. *The Encyclopedia of Ghosts.* Dodd, Mead, 1984.

Coleman, Nadine Mills. *Mistress of Ravenswood.* Columbia Daily Tribune, 1992.

Combs, Loula Long. *My Revelation.* Longview Publishing Company, 1947.

Dufur, Brett, and Jim Borwick. *Forgotten Missourians Who Made History.* Pebble Publishing, 1996.

Ebon, Martin, ed. *Communicating With the Dead.* New American Library, 1891–1968.

Edwards, Frank. *Strange People.* Popular Library, 1961.

Ellis, Jerry. *Bareback.* Thorndike Press, 1994.

Enright, D. J., ed. *The Oxford Book of Death.* Oxford University Press, 1983.

Gaddis, Vincent H. *Mysterious Fires and Lights.* David McCay, 1967.

Ghost Hunting, Professional Haunted House Investigation. Aires Production, 1988.

Glancy, Diane. *Pushing the Bear.* Harcourt Brace, 1996.

Guiley, Rosemary Ellen. *The Encyclopedia of Ghosts and Spirits.* Facts on File, 1992.

Hale, Allean Lemon. *Petticoat Pioneer.* North Central Publishing, 1956–1968.

Hauck, Dennis William. *The National Directory of Haunted Places.* Athanor Press, 1994.

Hickman, Irene. *I Knew Patience Worth.* 2d ed. Hickman Systems New Age Books, 1995.

———. *Remote Depossession.* Hickman Systems New Age Books, 1994.

Hill, Douglas, and Pat Williams. *The Supernatural.* Hawthorn, 1965.

Jaegers, Bevy C. *Psychometry: The Science of Touch.* Aires Productions, 1980.

Jarvis, Sharon, ed. *Dead Zones.* Warner Books, 1992.

Jones, Linda Newcomb. *The Longview We Remember.* Storm Ridge Press, 1991.

Litvag, Irving. *Singer in the Shadows: The Strange Story of Patience Worth.* Popular Library, 1972.

Macklin, John. *Casebook of the Unknown.* Ace Books, 1974.

Manley, Seon, and Gogo Lewis. *Baleful Beasts.* Lothrop, Lee and Shepard, 1974.

May, Antoinette. *Psychic Women.* Hickman Systems, 1984.

Mitchell, Clarence Dewey. *Jim, the Wonder Dog.* Jim the Wonder Dog, Inc., 1942–1989.

Moore, Thomas. *Mysterious Tales and Legends of the Ozarks.* Dorrance, 1938.

Neider, Charles, ed. *The Autobiography of Mark Twain.* Harper and Row, 1975.

Norman, Michael, and Beth Scott. *Historic Haunted America.* TOR, 1995.
——. *Noted Witnesses for Psychic Occurrences.* University Books, 1963.
The Oxford Dictionary of Quotations. 2d and 3d eds. Oxford University Press, 1953, 1980.
Packard, Vance. *The Human Side of Animals.* Pocket Books, 1961.
Prince, Walter Franklin. *The Case of Patience Worth.* University Books, 1927–1964.
Randolph, Vance. *Ozark Magic and Folklore.* Columbia University Press, 1947; facsimile by Dover, 1964.
Rogo, D. Scott. *An Experience of Phantoms.* Taplinger Publishing, 1974.
Schurmacher, Emile C. *Strange Unsolved Mysteries.* Paperback Library, 1967.
Scott, Beth and Michael Norman. *Haunted Heartland.* Dorset Press, 1985.
Sherman, Harold. *You Live After Death.* Fawcett, 1972.
Smith, Alson J. *Immortality: The Scientific Evidence.* Prentice Hall, 1954.
Steele, Phillip. *Ozark Tales and Superstitions.* Pelican Publishing, 1983.
Steiner, Rudolph. *Reincarnation and Karma.* Anthroposophic Press, 1962.
Stewart, Melinda, ed. *Old Settler's Gazette: Legends of the Ozarks.* Updated, 1970s.
Strong, Julia Bernard. *Letters, 1836–1839.* Unpublished. Joint Collection Western Historical Manuscript Collection, State Historical Society of Missouri Manuscripts. Ellis Hall, University of Missouri-Columbia.
True Experiences With Ghosts. New American Library, 1968.
Tweedale, Violet. *Ghosts I Have Seen and Other Psychic Experiences.* Herbert Jenkins (London), 1920.
USA Weekend. *I Never Believed in Ghosts Until...100 Real-Life Encounters.* Barnes and Noble, 1992.
van Ravenswaay, Charles. Introduction. *The WPA Guide to 1930s Missouri.* University Press of Kansas, 1936–1986.
Walker, Stephen P. *Lemp: A Haunting History.* The Lemp Preservation Society, 1988.

Magazine Articles

Berry, Heather. "Specter, Spirit or Spoof?" *Rural Missouri,* October 1989.
Coleman, Nadine Mills. "Mistress of Ravenswood." *Missouri Life,* September–October 1973.
Cox, Vicki. "Ellen Gray Massey, Romancing the Ozarks." *Ozarks Senior Living,* September 1994.
Gilbert, Joan. "The House the Ghost Loved." *Fate Magazine,* January 1988.
——. "Ozarks Mountaineer: A Few Ozarks Ghosts." *Missouri Life,* September–October 1991.
——. "Patience Worth, Ghostly Writer." *Rural Missouri,* January 1981.
Gilbert, Joan, and Jacki Gray. "The Ghosts of Missouri, Past and Present." *Missouri Life,* December 1984.
"The Hornet Ghost Light." No author. *Harbinger Magazine,* 1970.
Kennedy, Carmen. "Ravenswood." *Missouri Life,* December 1985.
Mason, Tom. "The Legends of a Haunted Bridge." *Springfield!* October 1985.
Shannon, Christine. "Ghosts in the Country." *Almanac for Farmers and City Folk,* 1993.
"Terrifying Tales of Nine Haunted Houses." No author. *Life Magazine,* November 1980.
Vance, Joel E. "A Couple of Well Known Dogs." *Missouri Conservationist,* December 1990.

Vest, Lawrence, Margaret Nelson Stephens, and Marian M. Ohman. "Missouri's Turn of the Century First Couple." *Missouri Historical Review,* April 1997.

Wilson, Suzanne J. "Spooklight." *Missouri Conservationist,* January 1997.

Wood, Larry E. "The Hornet Spook Light." *Missouri Life,* September–October 1977.

Woodward, Eva Marie. "Agatha's Dutch Oven." *Fate Magazine.* Undated clip.

Newspaper Articles

Ansley, Leslie. "Hannibal, Missouri." *USA Weekend,* August 16–18, 1991.

Armstrong, Jennie. "Mrs. M.: A Spirited Guest at KC Hotel." *Kansas City Star,* April 10, 1985.

Bargman, Joe. "Spirits in the House." *Columbia Daily Tribune,* October 25, 1987.

Barnes, Harper. "Where Spirits Walk." *St. Louis Post-Dispatch,* January 26, 1977.

Bauer, Traci. "Haunted Hills." *Springfield Daily News,* October 27, 1996.

Bell, Sara. "Party Benefits Heritage." *Columbia Missourian,* June 26, 1996.

Bennish, Steven. "Stephens Spirit." *Columbia Daily Tribune,* August 20, 1986.

"Bloodland's Residents May Still Linger." No byline. *Daily Gateway Guide,* October 30, 1975.

Botel, Helen. "Spook Story Explained." *Springfield Daily News,* October 16, 1968.

Bowles, Lee Ann. "Ghostly Romance." *Columbia Missourian,* September 14, 1986.

Breckenridge, D. P. "Ghostly Prey Elusive at James Farm." *Kansas City Star,* January 26, 1982.

Charton, Scott. "Born of Compromise." *Columbia Daily Tribune,* August 11, 1966.

"The Chase Hotel: The Tradition Lives On." No byline. *St. Louis Post-Dispatch,* May 3, 1985.

Clayton, Joe. "Ethereal Figures Vanish as Ozarks' Past Fades." *Springfield Daily News,* October 12, 1981.

Creighton, Jim. "Ghosts in St. Louis Lack Character." *St. Louis Post-Dispatch,* April 6, 1975.

——. "Psychic St. Louis." *St. Louis Post-Dispatch.* Nine-part series ending late September 1977.

Curnutt, Kirk. "Ravenswood." *Columbia Missourian,* May 17, 1987.

Dames, Joan Foster. "West End Family Thinks Ghost May Inhabit House." *St. Louis Post-Dispatch,* January 11, 1967.

Davis, Jean, column ed. "Over the Ozarks." *Springfield Daily News,* June 2, 1977.

Dengler, John. "The Ghosts of Main Street." *St. Charles Living,* February 7, 1997. B. C. by William Stafford.

"Do Ghosts Like You?" No byline. *Springfield Daily News,* October 1978, *undated clip.*

Flanigan, Susan. "Is Columbia Haunted by G-G-Ghosts?" *Columbia Missourian,* October 28, 1984.

Foster, Al. "Mark Twain's Home Town." *St. Louis Post-Dispatch,* April 19, 1981.

Funkhouser, Clifford. "Death Rode the Rails." *Marceline Press,* July 23, 1973.

Futterman, Ellen. "The Splendors and the Mysteries of Ravenswood." *St. Louis Post-Dispatch,* May 11, 1986.

"Ghostly Town." *Hannibal Courier-Post,* November 4, 1996.

"Ghosts Roam Pre–Civil War Mansion." *Daily Gateway Guide,* January 1977.

Gilbert, Joan. "The Historic Lure of Ravenswood Mansion." *Columbia Senior Times,* September 1996.

"A Haunted Hotel." No byline. *Missouri Patriot*, September 9, 1875.

"The Haunting History of the Lemp Family." By "Staff member of the P.D." *St. Louis Post-Dispatch*, March 18, 1990.

Hernon, Peter. "Ozark Spook Light: Fact or Fantasy?" *St. Louis Globe Democrat*, November 15-16, 1980.

"History Is Alive and Well in St. Charles." No byline. *St. Louis Globe Democrat*, July 1, 1978.

Houston, Brant. "Ghosts: A Dark Quest for the Unearthly." *Kansas City Star*, October 30, 1981.

Hughes, John. "Tales of the Truly Weird." *Kansas City Star Magazine*, October 25, 1987.

Hunter, Max. "Ghostly Stories Abound in Ozarks." *Springfield Daily News*, October 31, 1980.

"Hunting Real Ghosts." No byline. *St. Louis Post-Dispatch*, May 4, 1988.

Krause, Betsy. "A Haunting Season." *Columbia Daily Tribune*, July 25, 1988.

Ladwig, Tom. "Breadtray Has a Slice of History." *Columbia Daily Tribune*, undated.

——. "Well Known Boonville Ghost." *Columbia Missourian*, September 27, 1987.

LaRouche, Robert. "Bingham's Arrow Rock." *St. Louis Post-Dispatch*, October 30, 1996.

——. "New Blends With Old in St. Charles." *St. Louis Post-Dispatch*, October 6, 1968.

Levin, Myron. "Ghostly Things Keep Feet, Tongues Moving." *Kansas City Star*, May 27, 1979.

Maneke, Jean. "Things That Go Bump in the Landers." *Springfield Daily News*, September 15, mid-70s, *undated clip*.

Meyers, Jeff. "Spirit of Lemp House." *St. Louis Post-Dispatch*, September 2, 1979.

Michael, Prince of Greece. "Have You Ever Seen a Ghost?" *Parade Magazine*, August 20, 1995.

O'Brien, Mike. "Ha'nts of Old Still Float Through Ozark Mountains." *Springfield Daily News*, October 28, 1996.

Randolph, Vance. "Lowlander, Collecting a Legacy." *Springfield Daily News*, August 17, 1975.

"Ravenswood, Reflection of Times Gone By." No byline. *The OATS Wheel*, January 1987.

"Realtors Seek Haunted House Guidelines." No byline. *Columbia Daily Tribune*, June 6, 1991.

Rice, Jack. "X-Rated Hannibal of Twain's Day." *St. Louis Post-Dispatch*, July 22, 1973.

Sauer, Georgia. "The Castle: Mystery in the West End." *St. Louis Post-Dispatch*, September 3, 1989.

Scarborough, Roger. "Murdered Traveler's Ghost Is Said to Haunt Local House." *Daily Gateway Guide*, October 31, 1980.

"St. Louis, Happy Haunting for Halloween." No byline. *St. Louis Globe Democrat*, October 27, 1978.

Stiffler, Dee. "Haunts, Horrors or Hoaxes." *Columbia Missourian*, October 30, 1992.

Summerhays, Sara. "Bleak House." *Columbia Daily Tribune*, April 14, 1991.

"Weird Tale of Ghost in West End." No byline. *St. Louis Post-Dispatch*, June 1, 1906.

Whitman, Arthur. "Vestige of a Genteel Past." *St. Louis Post-Dispatch*, May 17, 1964.

Yates, Junait. "Garth Mansion, One of Twain's Favorites." *Mark Twain Lake Guide*, June 4, 1984.

——. "Rockcliffe Mansion." *Mark Twain Lake Guide*, June 6, 1984.

About the Author

J oan Gilbert's most recent book is a University of Missouri release titled *Trail of Tears across Missouri,* which is part of the Missouri Heritage Readers Series. This book won first prizes for work done in 1996 by members of the Missouri Writers Guild and Missouri Press Women. It also won second prize from the National Federation of Press Women. Earlier Joan wrote two other novels. She has sold more than 600 pieces of short nonfiction and several short stories. Her markets are mainly horse publications and those concerned with history and rural living.

Joan was born and grew up in Dixon, Missouri, and received her B.S. from Southwest Missouri State Missouri University in Springfield. Today she lives near Hallsville, where she continues writing books and and articles.

Index

The Show Me Missouri Series

99 Fun Things to Do in Columbia & Boone County
Guide to hidden highlights, galleries, museums, towns, people and history in Columbia, Rocheport, Centralia and Boone County. Most trips are free or under $10. Includes maps and photos. 168 pages. By Pamela Watson. $12.95. ISBN: 0-9646625-2-3

A to Z Missouri—A dictionary-style book of Missouri place name origins
Abo to Zwanzig! Includes history, pronunciations, population, county, post office dates and more. 220 pages. By Margot Ford McMillen. $14.95. ISBN: 0-9646625-4-X

The Complete Katy Trail Guidebook—America's longest Rails-to-Trails Project
The definitive guide to services, towns, people, places and history along Missouri's 200-mile Katy Trail. This third edition covers the cross-state hiking and biking trail from Clinton to St. Charles. Includes maps, 80 photos and more. 168 pages. By Brett Dufur. $14.95. ISBN: 0-9646625-0-7

Daytrip Missouri—The tour guide standard for Missouri
Includes annual events, travel tips, 60 photos and 20 maps. 224 pages. By Lee N. Godley and Patricia Murphy O'Rourke. $14.95. ISBN: 0-9651340-0-8

Exploring Missouri Wine Country
This guidebook profiles wineries, including how to get there, their histories, wine tips, home-brew recipes, dictionary of wine terms and more. Also lists nearby bed & breakfasts, services and state parks. 192 pages. By Brett Dufur. $14.95. ISBN: 0-9646625-6-6

Forgotten Missourians Who Made History
A book of short stories and humorous comic-style illustrations of more than 35 Missourians who made a contribution to the state or nation yet are largely forgotten by subsequent generations. Compiled by Jim Borwick and Brett Dufur. $14.95. ISBN: 0-9646625-8-2

Missouri Ghosts—Spirits, Haunts & Related Lore
A lifetime's collection of spirits, haunts and folklore from around the state. This intriguing book highlights more than a century of Missouri's most spine-chilling and unexplainable phenomena. By Joan Gilbert. 230 pages. $14.95

River Rat's Guide to Missouri River Folklore and History
A Missouri River classic, documented bend by bend by river rat and historian Cecil Griffith. First published in 1974. Reissued with new maps and more. 144 pages. $14.95

The River Revisited—Reflections In the Wake of Lewis and Clark
Includes excerpts from the original voyage, as well as modern-day commentary from the 200 years since Lewis and Clark. Includes pull-out map of the Missouri River, 50 photos and journals from a modern-day crew of reenactors. 224 pages. By Brett Dufur. $16.95. ISBN: 0-9646625-9-0

Wit & Wisdom of Missouri's Country Editors
More than 600 pithy sayings from pioneer Missouri papers. Many of these quotes and quips date to the 19th century yet remain timely for today's readers. Richly illustrated and fully indexed to help you find that perfect quote. 168 pages. By William Taft. $14.95

Show Me Missouri books are available at many local bookstores. They can also be ordered directly from the publisher, using this form, or ordered by phone, fax or over the Internet.

Pebble Publishing also distributes 100 other books of regional interest, rails-to-trails, Missouri history, heritage, nature, recreation and more. These are available through our online bookstore and mail-order catalog.

Visit our online bookstore, *Trailside Books,* on the Internet at Trailsidebooks.com. If you would like to receive our free catalog, please fill out and mail the form on this page.

Pebble Publishing

P.O. Box 431 ❖ Columbia, MO 65205-0431
1 (800) 576-7322 ❖ Fax: (573) 698-3108

Quantity	*Book Title*	*x Unit Price*	*=Total*

Mo. residents add 6.975% sales tax = _____

Shipping ($2 first book, $1 each additional book) x = _____

Total = _____

☐ $2 enclosed for wildflower seed packet (book order not required)

Name:_____

Email Address:_____

Address:_____ Apt._____

City, State, Zip _____

Phone: (____) _____

Credit Card # _____

Expiration Date _____/_____/_____ Please send catalog _____

Visit *Trailside Books* online at Trailsidebooks.com

ℰℴ   Reading this book of ghostly happenings gives the reader the perfect opportunity to shiver a little or perhaps giggle a bit over the tales. . .In recording them, Gilbert has done a great service for Missouri history and the preservation of local folklore.

— Dorothy H. Shrader, author of
Steamboat Legacy and *Steamboat Treasures*

ℰℴ   I truly enjoyed it. . .particularly the ghost stories about Hannibal. It was neat to recognize the names and places that were written about. . . The read was fun and easy.

— Emily Danielsons, Hannibal 7th-grader

ℰℴ   Joan Gilbert, who had written for national magazines for many years, here presents Missouri's "ghost facts" as she found them, summarizing meticulous research honestly and entertainingly. Whether true or myth, her Missouri ghost stories are too good to miss.

— Sue Gerard, columnist, author and potter

ℰℴ   What Charles Guenther's *Missouri Woods* is to regional poetry, Joan Gilbert's *Missouri Ghosts* is to its genre.

— William Barnaby Faherty, Society of Jesus